ORGANIZING THE EARLY LITERACY CLASSROOM

The Essential Library of PreK–2 Literacy

Sharon Walpole and Michael C. McKenna, *Series Editors*
www.guilford.com/PK2

Supporting the literacy development of our youngest students plays a crucial role in later academic achievement. Grounded in research and theory, this series provides a core collection of practical, accessible resources for every teacher, administrator, and staff developer in the early grades. Books in the series contain a wealth of lesson plans, case examples, assessment guidelines, and links to the Common Core State Standards. Issues specific to each grade—and the essential teaching and learning connections between grades—are discussed. Reproducible materials in each volume are available online for purchasers to download and print in a convenient 8½″ × 11″ size.

Organizing the Early Literacy Classroom

HOW TO PLAN FOR SUCCESS AND REACH YOUR GOALS

Sharon Walpole
Michael C. McKenna

THE GUILFORD PRESS
New York   London

Copyright © 2016 The Guilford Press
A Division of Guilford Publications, Inc.
370 Seventh Avenue, Suite 1200, New York, NY 10001
www.guilford.com

Printed in the United States of America

This book is printed on acid-free paper.

Last digit is print number: 9 8 7 6 5 4 3 2 1

Library of Congress Cataloging-in-Publication Data

Names: Walpole, Sharon, author. | McKenna, Michael C., author.
Title: Organizing the early literacy classroom : how to plan for success and
   reach your goals / Sharon Walpole, Michael C. McKenna.
Description: New York, NY : The Guilford Press, 2016. | Series: The essential
   library of preK-2 literacy | Includes bibliographical references and index.
Identifiers: LCCN 2016006016| ISBN 9781462526536 (hardcover : acid-free
   paper) | ISBN 9781462526529 (paperback : acid-free paper)
Subjects: LCSH: Reading (Preschool) | Reading (Elementary) | Classroom
   management. | Classroom environment. | BISAC: EDUCATION / Classroom
   Management. | LANGUAGE ARTS & DISCIPLINES / Study & Teaching. | EDUCATION
   / Teaching Methods & Materials / Reading & Phonics. | LANGUAGE ARTS &
   DISCIPLINES / Literacy.
Classification: LCC LB1140.5.R4 W35 2016 | DDC 372.4—dc23
LC record available at https://lccn.loc.gov/2016006016

About the Authors

Sharon Walpole, PhD, is Professor in the School of Education at the University of Delaware. She has extensive school-based experience designing and implementing tiered instructional programs. Dr. Walpole has also been involved in federally funded and other schoolwide reform projects. Her current work focuses on the design and effects of schoolwide reforms, particularly those involving literacy coaches. She has coauthored or coedited several other books with Michael C. McKenna, including *How to Plan Differentiated Reading Instruction: Resources for Grades K–3* and *The Literacy Coach's Handbook, Second Edition,* and she is coauthor of *The Building Blocks of Preschool Success* with Katherine A. Beauchat and Katrin L. Blamey. Dr. Walpole is a recipient of the Early Career Award for Significant Contributions to Literacy Research and Education from the Literacy Research Association.

Michael C. McKenna, PhD, is Thomas G. Jewell Professor of Reading in the Curry School of Education at the University of Virginia. He has authored, coauthored, or edited more than 20 books, including *Assessment for Reading Instruction, Third Edition,* and over 100 articles, chapters, and technical reports on a range of literacy topics. Dr. McKenna's research has been supported by the National Reading Research Center and the Center for the Improvement of Early Reading Achievement. He is a corecipient of the Edward B. Fry Book Award from the Literacy Research Association and the Award for Outstanding Academic Books from the American Library Association.

Series Editors' Note

Whether you are a first-year teacher or a seasoned veteran, it pays to reflect on the tools of your craft. We are not referring to your knowledge of instructional approaches or to your expertise in assessing the needs of your students. The other books in The Essential Library of PreK–2 Literacy series do an excellent job of addressing these needs. Instead, we invite you to step back and think carefully about how prepared you are to implement those approaches.

Being prepared means more than knowing how to teach effectively. It means being organized. The organized teacher knows exactly which books and materials are available and is able locate them quickly. She arranges the classroom in a safe and logical way. The organized teacher maintains records of student progress in order to plan instruction appropriately and report grades accurately. He understands the roles played by other professionals and works collaboratively with them as part of a team.

Our hope is that this book, the cornerstone volume of The Essential Library, will offer a framework for evaluating your own organization together with suggestions for improving it. In Chapter 1, we underscore the importance of having clear goals to guide your teaching, both for your class and for individual students. All of the decisions you make must reflect these goals, and achieving them must be reflected in turn in your organization. We also urge you to develop another set of goals as well—for yourself. As your students' learning progresses, so should your own professional learning. One should inform the other. In Chapter 2, we extend our discussion of professional learning by discussing how to assemble a library of resources, including both a "starter set" of books and a range of free online education resources.

The next three chapters address issues arising from the new standards. In Chapter 3, we discuss how the literacy curriculum should align with the heightened expectations of the Common Core State Standards (and the revised standards of nonadopting states), and we then describe how you can take stock of the materials and methods you are using, including technology resources. In Chapter 4, we approach standards from the perspective of the assessments needed to gauge student progress and identify instructional needs. We examine the question of which assessments are likely to provide the data you need and which are not. In Chapter 5, we extend the use of assessment data to standards-based report cards, a topic of emerging importance.

The next four chapters concern important but frequently overlooked dimensions of organization. Chapter 6 contains evidence-based suggestions for organizing classroom space, a topic with surprising implications for instructional effectiveness. In Chapter 7, we turn to the subject of professional relationships and the vital importance of collaborating with specialists and other colleagues in a coordinated manner. In Chapter 8, we offer guidance for organizing your time, perhaps the most valuable commodity you have to spend. In light of the many demands you face, our guiding principle is to accomplish as much as you can in the time you have. We offer guidance on how to accomplish this end. In Chapter 9, we make a case for organizing the books in your classroom, not only to make it easier to locate them but also to evaluate the quality and range of your classroom library. We present detailed checklists to help you take stock.

In the final two chapters, we explore additional ways in which being organized can enhance your effectiveness as a teacher of young children. The first is establishing routines. In Chapter 10, we explore the reasons for explicitly teaching instructional routines as a means of saving time, maintaining focus, ensuring efficient transitions, and facilitating classroom management. In the last chapter, we turn to parents and offer suggestions for organizing the ways in which you can clearly and continually communicate with them, not only to keep them informed but to secure their support as true partners in the literacy development of their children.

Finally, a general note about The Essential Library of PreK–2 Literacy. We are absolutely delighted with the books our colleagues have contributed to this series (see them listed in Figure 2.4). Our confidence in their expertise has been richly rewarded, as each author team has achieved just the right balance between presenting the research evidence and describing the instructional strategies that emanate from it. We firmly believe that the seven books in this series will provide an excellent basis for your continued professional learning. Happy reading!

SHARON WALPOLE, PhD
MICHAEL C. MCKENNA, PhD

Contents

CHAPTER 1

· · · · · · · · · · · ·

Setting Teaching
and Learning Goals

GUIDING QUESTIONS

- How can standards help you to set learning goals?
- How can you combine information from standards with knowledge of development to set up a classroom assessment plan?
- What assessments are essential at each of the early primary grades?
- How can you make a reasonable plan for conducting assessments and using the results?
- How can you set goals for your own learning?

As we write, a new school year is starting all around us. Many parents are grudgingly getting back into bedtime and bus routines, some of them for the first time. Children are settling in to classrooms with new peers and new expectations. More importantly, though, teachers, both novice and experienced, are building new classroom communities and new communities of practice with their peers. As we have engaged in these processes with teachers over the years, we have seen both the promise of the new year and its perils. We have witnessed first-hand the research finding that "grit, defined as passion and perseverance for long-term goals, predicts both teacher retention and effectiveness" (Robertson-Craft & Duckworth, 2014, p. 22). In this chapter, we will be "beginning with the end in mind" (Covey, 1989). We want to enhance your chances for a great year so that you will find teaching a long and rewarding career.

Let's start with some facts. Figure 1.1 provides a visual.

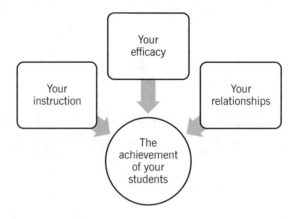

FIGURE 1.1. Teacher effectiveness, efficacy, and collaborations.

- Your personal work in your own classroom, more than your years of experience or your academic training, matters to the achievement of your students, both this year and in the future (Rivkin, Hanushek, & Kain, 2005).
- Your self-efficacy, your beliefs that you can perform the tasks required of your job well and that you can personally influence the achievement of your children, regardless of their backgrounds, matters to the achievement of your students. Your positive beliefs about the efficacy of the teachers you work with also matters (Goddard, Hoy, & Hoy, 2000).
- The relationships that you build with peers and administrators in your school matter to your feelings of efficacy (Pas, Bradshaw, & Hershfeldt, 2012).

Because we know that these things matter, it makes sense for us to foster them. In this book, we will do that by sharing lessons that we have learned from other researchers and from the many teachers, teacher leaders, and administrators we have worked with in the field. We will argue that instruction, efficacy, and relationships can be enhanced by a coherent organizational plan. So let's get started.

Setting Goals for Learning

In the early primary classroom, teachers with high levels of personal efficacy set goals for their children based on standards while they attend to students as individuals capable of growth. Perhaps that is the underlying mechanism by which efficacy and achievement are related. Standards can be very useful here. While efforts to enact consistent standards across states have proved controversial, we have no quarrel with the content of the Common Core State Standards (CCSS; National

Governors Association Center for Best Practices & Council of Chief State School Officers [NGA & CCSSO], 2010). In fact, we see them as potentially powerful levers to accelerate children's early reading performance *and* enhance their background and vocabulary knowledge from the first years of school.

Let's look at the CCSS conceptually first. Figure 1.2 provides an overview of the topics included in the Standards. Think about whether an early primary teacher would quarrel, in general, about considering any one of these an important target. Who doesn't want children to grow in their foundational skills? In their ability to speak and listen? In their achievement as readers and writers of different types of text? Then think about whether you find it realistic to devise your own goals in each of these areas. We don't. We tend to take standards at face value to help us to organize our time, our resources, and our expectations. Standards, in any form, allow you to "begin with the end in mind" and plan your work. We will get more specific in later chapters, but we think your goals for student literacy learning should be informed by the standards in your state.

Preschool teachers are in a challenging spot. The CCSS start in kindergarten, but preschool teachers work with children before that milestone. Are they

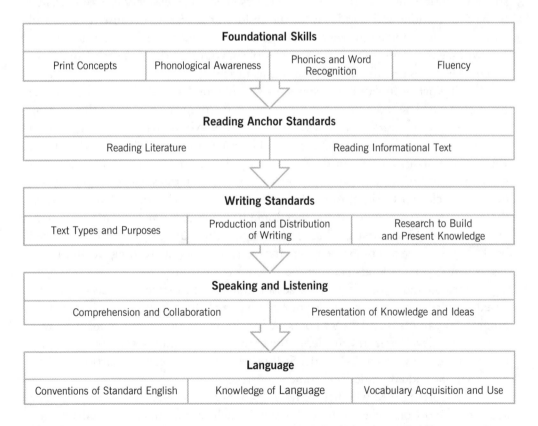

FIGURE 1.2. Overview of the Common Core State Standards for the English Language Arts.

without standards? Not exactly. There are early childhood standards in many states. Research in preschool identifies very specific areas as targets: print concepts, phonological awareness, beginning alphabet knowledge, emergent writing, and many aspects of speaking, listening, and language. Those connections to CCSS are easy to see. What may be less visible (but more exciting!) is the potential for engaging preschoolers in higher-level thinking. Early childhood educators (see, e.g., Hoffman, Paciga, & Teale, 2014) applaud emphasis on knowledge building through interactive read-alouds of more complex narrative informational text and on writing, but they remind preschool teachers not to lose sight of developmentally appropriate and play-based settings. We recommend that preschool teachers consider kindergarten standards and early learning standards in their state and focus on including the high-level outcomes of language, knowledge, and writing—not foundational skills that will be more easily developed in kindergarten.

Using Data to Size Up a Class

Once you know your overall standards-based goals, it makes sense to assess your students' initial status. Early primary teachers need an assessment toolkit matched to the expectations and standards for the children they teach. Because reading and writing are developmental, we fill that toolkit differently at different grade levels. You will see that some of the assessment tools in your toolkit are more formal than others. The tools are identified by emphasis in Figure 1.3.

Don't worry—it is unlikely that your school won't already have most of these bases covered. The most important first step is to conduct an audit of the existing (and especially the *required*) assessments (Stahl & McKenna, 2013). Go beyond the names and ask yourself what aspects of literacy are actually being assessed and whether any assessments can do double duty. For example, many schools use a storybook reading task at the beginning of kindergarten to assess concepts of print (front to back, left to right, top to bottom, and concept of word). If you recorded the assessment, you could also gather some baseline data on speaking, listening, and language. Many first- and second-grade teachers are required to use leveled book assessments of comprehension. If you recorded oral reading during those assessments, you could also garner words correct in 1 minute.

After you audit your required assessments for their match to these standards-based requirements, think about your report card. In our experience, reporting progress to parents is still a very hot issue in schools. Some schools report progress only, with a developmental rubric, in the early primary grades. Others have fairly traditional grades on an A–F scale. Still others have a mastery reporting system, with each individual grade-level standard listed.

We are often asked whether we favor standards-based mastery reporting. Our answer is, "Sort of." The nature of literacy is such that foundational skills can be mastered, and they can be mastered by all children on time. They are what Scott

	Foundational Skills	Reading	Writing	Speaking and Listening	Language
PreK	Concepts-of-print assessment Rhyme recognition task Alphabet recognition		Drawing prompt	Dialogic reading, audio recorded	
K	Concepts-of-print assessment Letter-name task Letter-sound task Phonemic segmentation and blending task Consonant–vowel–consonant decoding task Consonant–vowel–consonant spelling task		Handwriting sample Writing prompt	Dialogic reading, audio recorded	
1	Letter-sound task Phonemic segmentation and blending task Decoding inventory Spelling inventory High-frequency word inventory Oral reading fluency task	Story-mapping task Informational text retell task	Handwriting sample Writing prompt	Informal assessment during read-alouds	
2	Decoding inventory Spelling inventory High-frequency word inventory Oral reading fluency task	Story-mapping task Informational text retell task	Writing prompt	Informal assessment during read-alouds	

FIGURE 1.3. PreK–2 assessment toolkit.

Paris (2005) calls "constrained" skills. It makes good sense to report progress at the mastery level on those skills. Concepts of print, phonemic awareness, decoding and word recognition, and even most aspects of fluency are constrained. Reading comprehension, writing, speaking and listening, and language are unconstrained skills. They develop over a lifetime; they are never "mastered." These areas are not well matched to mastery-learning or standards-based reporting.

Classroom Goals

We view early-year assessments of both constrained and unconstrained skills as variables in an algebraic distance equation. The unknown to solve for is the amount of progress that you must foster, collectively for your class and individually for each student, through your teaching efforts. Either directly or conceptually, initial assessments help you to get a sense of the learning distance to be traveled by your students. Once you know where you need to go, you can better allocate time and attention. Generally, with all data, you have to collect it quickly, summarize it logically, and think about it. Of course, that is easier said than done.

As schools have institutionalized response-to-intervention (RTI) frameworks, they have increasingly adopted assessments that allow teachers to identify levels of risk for students. You will often see assessments of constrained skills reported this way. DIBELS, the Dynamic Indicators of Basic Early Literacy Skills, are a good example. Some portion of students score at benchmark, both within and across subtests. That means that given their score at this time of year and their access to instruction, they are "on track" for meeting end-of-year goals. Some portion of students have scores that are called "strategic" or "some risk." That means that given access to regular instruction, they may or may not meet end-of-year goals; it may be wise to keep a close eye on them and to provide some additional support. The remaining children's scores yield the label "intensive." Without some opportunities in addition to regular instruction, they are highly unlikely to meet end-of-year goals.

We recently met with grade-level teams in an elementary school to review their beginning-of-the-year data for constrained skills. Figure 1.4 presents a visual summary.

These data present a powerful picture, and it is both retrospective and prospective. Retrospectively, here is the story: Most children (72%) entered kindergarten with strong foundational skills. In this case, we also knew that 60% of them had attended preschool, and teachers reported that that trend was associated with better beginning-of-year scores. Only a third of the children who entered first grade were on track, however; unless a large number of children transferred

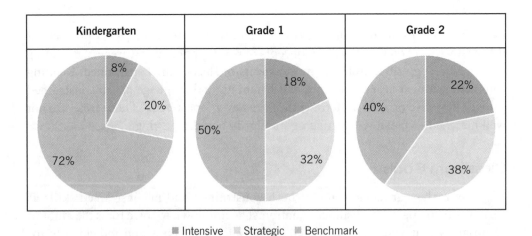

FIGURE 1.4. Grade-level data, beginning of year.

from different schools, their kindergarten experience was not successful in the areas assessed in early first grade. By second grade, a slightly larger percentage of children were beginning the year on track, but at the same time a slightly larger number were beginning with intensive needs. Our advice was to reexamine the organization of the curriculum in kindergarten and to plan for immediate interventions in first and second grade.

Looking prospectively, the kindergarten team was working from a position of strength. They had small numbers of children requiring immediate intervention, and they could manage that while accelerating the already strong development of the majority of the children. For first-grade teachers, a small number of children at benchmark was expanded by the number with strategic needs to 82%. That led us to recommend that teachers provide a quick review of foundational skills for all and then attend to rigorous grade-level instruction. We also planned for intervention times for the children with intensive needs (18%). The same general pattern yielded the same recommendations for second grade. We also suggested that students be tracked from the beginning of the year to the middle and end in order to monitor the trends at each grade.

The picture is fuzzier with unconstrained skills. That is because those skills are harder to assess quickly and easily, and the results don't conform to the numerical scales. They are better viewed qualitatively, with rubrics and descriptors. We think writing is the most important unconstrained skill for baseline assessment. You can collect a beginning-of-the-year writing sample fairly easily from your entire class. We have found the writing samples and assessments in the open-access website *achievethecore.org* to be a useful tool. You will see that there are writing prompts, beginning at kindergarten, that require you to read aloud a short text, engage your children in a natural discussion, and then draw and write to express an opinion or narrate a sequence of events. A series of dated writing samples collected under similar conditions will give you (and parents) a concrete picture of student performance over time. In the early years of school, these samples typically provide a compelling rationale for building the foundational skills (e.g., concept of print, phonemic awareness, alphabet knowledge, and handwriting) that underlie transcription (listening to oral language and writing it down). If children don't have the skills to put words to paper, they certainly can't compose coherent persuasive, informative, and narrative writing pieces.

Individual Goals

Once you have a sense of the overall make-up of your class, you have to think of students both in groups and one at a time. For constrained skills, this is easier, of course. And visuals help. Special educators have long used a tool called an aimline. It is simply an estimate of change over time in a specific skill. It is a line graph with scores along the vertical axis and time along the horizontal one. It shows that some students have to make more progress each week or month than others. Figure 1.5 provides a simple example. A kindergarten teacher knows that letter-sound knowledge is important. She also knows that she wants all children to master this constrained skill by the end of November so that she can use that foundational knowledge to facilitate writing. She sets an aimline to begin at 0 for the start of the year and end at 26 at the end of November. Then she plots student achievement against that aimline.

Student 1 began the year with 5 letter sounds. By October, he had gained an additional 13, putting his progress above the aimline. Instruction was clearly working for him, and the teacher anticipated that she would meet the November goal with the same level of support. Student 2 began with no letter sounds and had learned only 5 by October. Without a change in her rate of learning, she would not be likely to meet the end-of-November goal, so she needed additional support. In constrained skills, measured numerically, aimlines are a powerful visual tool to track progress and guide instruction.

For unconstrained skills, like listening or reading comprehension and composition, numerical representations of discrete skills are less helpful. Instead, work samples, scored with rubrics, provide a better visual. Sometimes these rubric scores can also be represented in numbers, as growth over time. For example, the state of Delaware has developed open-access text-based writing rubrics. The writing is scored in four domains (reading/research, development, organization, and language/conventions) with four possible ratings.

Figure 1.6 shows one student's work represented in each of these domains at three time points.

The graph reveals that the student is making strong progress toward a score of 4 in the areas of using research and reading, in development of an argument, and in language conventions. Organization is the problem area here and deserves special attention in writing conferences and in revisions. This type of data about

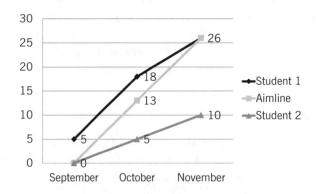

FIGURE 1.5. Aimline for letter sounds.

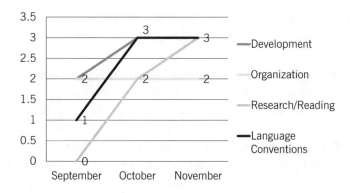

FIGURE 1.6. Student progress in persuasive writing.

writing is more useful when coupled with the actual writing sample so that all stakeholders (students, parents, and teachers) can see exactly what writing was associated with what rating.

A Classroom Example

This goal-setting business is a lot to envision. But it is also the normal work of preplanning time and the first weeks of school. Imagine Ms. Howard, a teacher with 3 years of experience in fifth grade, who transferred to first grade. She has to orient herself first to the differences in learning goals for students who are beginning readers. The foundational skills strand of the CCSS for first grade looks very concrete to her. She is accustomed to thinking about oral reading fluency as the only foundational skill to assess and track, but she sees from the standards that first-grade fluency is fueled by a very specific set of phonics and word recognition skills, which are in turn fueled by phonological awareness. She sees that the anchor standards in reading literature and information text are the same as the ones that she developed in fifth grade, but the grade-level indicators are very different. She sees very specific goals in speaking and listening and in language, but it is difficult for her to envision them in action because she has no experience with first graders.

Ms. Howard works with the first-grade team leader, Mrs. Farmer, to review the required assessments. She has to give the DIBELS Next battery, an informal decoding inventory, and a high-frequency word inventory. These required assessments seem well suited to cover the foundational skills, but she has no baseline assessment of reading or writing. She decides to add a task that she will use as a baseline for reading comprehension and for writing. She selects a simple narrative picture book. She decides she will read it aloud and then ask the children to draw about the beginning, middle, and end. Then she will ask them to write about the story for a classmate who didn't hear it. From this simple classroom task, she hopes to get a sense of what her children can do in listening comprehension, and in handwriting and spelling. She anticipates that she will have a lot of work to do in these areas.

After reviewing the standards and setting up her initial assessment toolkit, Ms. Howard makes a schedule. She would like to have all of the baseline assessments done in 4 weeks' time so that she can start differentiated instruction during week 5. She also reserves the first week of school to establish rituals and routines—no assessments. She sets specific goals: By the beginning of the second week of school, she will be providing whole-class English language arts (ELA) instruction for 45 minutes. Then she will have students working at their seats, drawing in response to reading, practicing their handwriting, taking turns at the computer station, and using her classroom library to browse information books and magazines. While students complete these tasks, she will call individuals back for the DIBELS battery. When she finishes with DIBELS, she will give the phonics inventory. At the beginning of week 3, she will administer her baseline writing assessment. Luckily, this one is whole class, so she can include it during instruction, and still make time for individual assessments that day.

Setting Goals for Teaching

As you will see in later chapters, we think scheduling and apportioning time for instruction is a key variable over which teachers must exert control. We also think that now is the time to be honest about the differences that rigorous new standards, regardless of their name in your state, require of us. If we look at the new standards conceptually, they are very exciting to us. And they *are* very different from previous standards and from previous practice. Much has been made of the shifts in text difficulty, with much more challenging text assigned to each grade level beginning in grade 2, and these shifts are real. However, there are more fundamental ones to consider in the early grades.

1. Building foundational skills is no longer the goal of the early primary years. Those skills are now positioned exactly where they should be—as low-level skills that children can master easily and quickly and on time. We can no longer teach them slowly or in dribs and drabs.
2. Building knowledge of all kinds is the most important goal of school. What children know (their background and vocabulary and language knowledge) is so directly linked to their reading and writing achievement that we must attend to knowledge building more systematically from the first day of preschool.
3. Writing is harder than reading, and writing achievement is now weighted equally with reading achievement in the standards. We have to link reading

with writing and we have to ensure that all children can write easily and early so that we can attend to the structure, content, and quality of their compositions.

We have been challenged in great new ways; we hope that you will join us.

Identifying Areas for Professional Growth

Remember that we began this chapter by reminding you that what you actually do in your classroom really does matter. The flip side is true as well: What you don't know or do matters too. Since standards are new and different, it doesn't make sense to argue that you were already doing these things or that you were well prepared in school to do them. They may not have been written when you were in school! Even if you graduated very recently, none of us in universities has fully grasped or enacted the standards even now. We are all learning together. And we are very excited about that.

"New Year's Resolutions": Making a Plan You Can Stick To

Many people make New Year's resolutions; few keep them. They are usually too numerous, too aggressive, too lofty, and made too quickly. "I'm going to be a more effective teacher this year" would fall into that category for us. What about these?

"I'm going to learn to accelerate foundational skills this year."
"I'm going to learn to use complex read-alouds to build knowledge this year."
"I'm going to learn how to teach handwriting and composition this year."

Any one of these might be a reasonable resolution. And over time, we hope many teachers will embrace all three. Notice, though, that these resolutions are about your own learning. That's what you can actually control. Of course, since your learning affects your teaching and your teaching affects your students, they will ultimately benefit.

Identifying a focus area is not enough. You do have to commit a portion of your scantest resource to the task. Learning new things requires a commitment of *time*. Lifelong learning requires the habit of learning. So start with what psychologists are calling a microhabit. A tiny step. What about this? Every Friday, before leaving school, commit to 15 minutes of reading in your goal area. If you do the 15 minutes, you will have met your goal. Over time, there will be days when you will lose yourself and spend an hour. Sometimes you will become really interested and read over the weekend. Some days you will come to school Monday with a really interesting idea to discuss with your teammates.

tting the Support You Need

Some people think that teachers can learn everything on the job. We are not among them. We believe that deep learning requires looking outside your classroom and school. We will be providing you with strategies for finding and using resources in the next chapter, so reading Chapter 2 can be your first Friday microhabit accomplishment!

Classroom Example

Ms. Howard, our first-grade teacher, was in for quite a shock when she collected her classroom writing sample. Most of her children only drew a picture, and even the pictures were uninterpretable to her fifth-grade-teacher eyes. She decided that she would focus on learning how to teach handwriting and writing. Since she had been working with us, she first went to our free professional learning website (*comprehensivereadingsolutions.com*) where she watched a module on teaching handwriting. Since the module contained a free curriculum for teaching handwriting, she was relieved. She Googled the author of the module, our colleague David Coker from the University of Delaware, and noted that he had written a new book, *Teaching Beginning Writers* (Coker & Ritchey, 2015), which she ordered.

Next she Googled first-grade writing samples, and saw a link to Reading Rockets, a site she trusted. When she followed that link, though, she was disheartened. The writing sample pictured was much better than any she had just collected, and the context section indicated that the children had just read a book by William Steig. None of her children could read that well yet. The next link she followed was more helpful. She saw that *achievethecore.org* had an extensive collection of writing samples and included commentary on what the children's writing revealed over time. She also saw writing prompts that she could use to judge progress. When she looked up, an hour had passed! She checked off her first week's microhabit progress as a yes in her plan book.

Summary

Organizing for instruction can have a powerful effect on you and on your students. Organizing begins with standards and assessment, and it includes goals for teaching and for your own professional learning. It may require you to rethink how you use time and resources in your classroom. We will work with you so that you can learn lessons from research and from the many teachers we've been working with. We share your commitment to early success for your classroom of young readers and writers.

CHAPTER 2
• • • • • • • • • • • •

Building a Professional Library

GUIDING QUESTIONS
....

- What are the crucial areas of early literacy instruction?
- Which areas provide you with the most opportunity for growth?
- What books have the most potential to help you learn?
- What free resources can you add to your professional library?
- How can you use your library to learn with your colleagues?
- How can you use your library to extend your personal learning?

Perhaps no one appreciates the value of learning more than a teacher. That is why the very best teachers we know never stop seeing themselves as learners. However, in the midst of an abundance of professional resources, it's important to be selective and focused concerning the kind of learning you pursue. Otherwise, you may find yourself adrift in a sea of information that may or may not help improve your classroom practice.

Making a List of Essential Topics
• •

The fact that you are reading a book on PreK–2 literacy indicates that you have taken the first step in narrowing the range of your professional learning objectives. But early literacy is still a very broad topic, and its many dimensions present a large number of choices. In addition, you are likely to be more knowledgeable about some areas than others, so it makes sense to prioritize your list of possible learning outcomes. You'll want to begin with areas about which you have limited knowledge but that can help your students the most. Figure 2.1 offers a self-assessment of

Topic	Your Level of Knowledge		
	Advanced	Intermediate	Limited
PreK–2 literacy standards			
Literacy interventions and RTI			
Writing			
Handwriting			
Word recognition			
Oral reading fluency			
Oral language and vocabulary			
Comprehension			
Differentiated instruction			
Shared reading			
Read-alouds			
Grammar instruction			

FIGURE 2.1. Self-assessment of early literacy knowledge. From *Organizing the Early Literacy Classroom: How to Plan for Success and Reach Your Goals* by Sharon Walpole and Michael C. McKenna. Copyright © 2016 The Guilford Press. Permission to photocopy this figure is granted to purchasers of this book for personal use or use with individual students (see copyright page for details). Purchasers can download enlarged versions of this figure (see the box at the end of the table of contents).

your professional knowledge. It is our position that all of the areas represented are instrumental in affecting student growth. In other words, we've taken the liberty of eliminating topics in which you may be interested but that are unlikely to be closely connected with student achievement. We would never discourage you from pursuing such topics, but there is more pressing business at hand.

Because we would never ask you to do something we wouldn't do ourselves, we took our own survey. It might surprise you to know that, for every topic, we rated our own knowledge as intermediate or limited. You might find this result surprising. After all, it's our job to stay current in these areas, and we have written entire books devoted to several of them. The fact is, however, that the more we learn about each of the components of early literacy instruction, the more we appreciate the limits of our knowledge. And that is precisely the perspective we hope you will adopt as you read the remainder of this book and other books in the series. Keep an open mind. Examine critically what you have believed to be true. And above all, embrace the role of learner.

Joining Forces with Peers

Let's begin with an important distinction. The role of learner is very different for adults than for the young children you teach (MacKeracher, 2004; McKenna & Walpole, 2008). Take off your primary teacher's hat for a moment and think about the last time you walked through a university library or entered a local coffee shop. It's likely that some of the adult learners you saw there were working alone—poring over devices, reading print books, or using both at the same time. Others were working together, sharing notes, discussing content, and helping each other understand. Which of these approaches is better? The short answer is, neither. You can accomplish a great deal by learning individually, but unless you interact with other learners, the knowledge you acquire may remain "academic" and unlikely to be applied in your classroom. Figure 2.2 illustrates the well-documented fact that acquiring knowledge about effective instructional practice does not automatically result in improved student outcomes (see Walpole & McKenna, 2013).

Learning Alone and Learning Together

Later in this chapter, we will recommend a number of books and other documents that we believe provide a good foundation for professional learning. To be clear from the start, we appreciate the fact that you are perfectly capable of comprehending these sources without the support of others. We have no doubt that you could read any of them and pass an examination. In our view, however, that is only the first step in meaningful professional development. The real goal is, or should be, far more ambitious. As Figure 2.2 suggests, it involves improved student learning as a result of altered instructional practice. Accomplishing this goal means more than reading about new approaches. It means implementing them, collecting data concerning their effectiveness, and reflecting on the results.

You can't take this step alone. It requires teamwork. This is true for a number of reasons. Being part of the team helps to ensure continuing motivation. (Think of going to the gym or eating healthily.) Team membership also provides opportunities to clarify the ideas presented by authors and to talk through possibilities for implementation. In the process, the team can become a sounding board for retrospective discussion. How well did it go? What problems arose? What successes did

FIGURE 2.2. The long road from teacher learning to student learning.

you experience? What modifications may be helpful? Is the new approach worth adopting on an extended basis? After working out a few logistics, team members are also in a position to observe one another, given the fact that they are starting with the same knowledge base. Figure 2.3 presents a slightly modified version of the peer coaching model devised by Joyce and Showers (2002; Showers & Joyce, 1996).

The final advantage of working together as a team is less tangible. It involves building a common set of expectations and a mutually agreed on vision of best practice—an instructional brand, if you will. Imagine all of the teachers at your grade level interviewing a job candidate. When the applicant asks about your approach to literacy instruction, would you need to respond that it depends on the teacher, or would you be able to say instead, "This is how we teach reading and writing in our school." You are not in this alone, after all. Having a shared set of beliefs and practices builds a positive climate, promotes professional communication, and ensures coherence across classrooms and grade levels.

Inventorying What You Have, Deciding What You Need

If you work as a team, two considerations are important from the outset. First, you must agree on what to read. Second, you must have multiple copies if you expect to study topics in a timely manner. If you have a common professional library (often located in a corner of the media center), you can quickly survey what is available. If you don't, then a meeting of team members for the purpose of bringing together your own professional books can accomplish the same purpose. (It may also reveal some of the preexisting beliefs of the various team members!) Either way, you can rather quickly compile a list of available print resources. The problem is choosing among them and making them available to all. A few guidelines may be helpful.

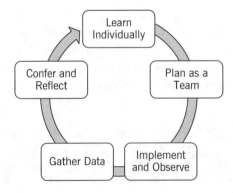

FIGURE 2.3. How teamwork can help ensure effective implementation.

- *Check the date.* Be certain you have the most current editions of books. You can find out quickly by visiting a publisher's website or by checking *Amazon. com* or Barnes & Noble online. Using the most current edition is not simply cosmetic. Under copyright law, a significant portion of a book's content must be new in order to qualify for a new edition. Consequently, you can rely upon authors to use the process of revision as a chance to update their books, correct errors, make important additions, and delete material that is outdated.

- *Be selective within a book.* Not every page of a book is likely to be of equal utility and relevance. This is especially true of edited volumes, in which different authors contribute chapters. Ultimately, a professional library will not simply consist of books but of portions of books on which team members agree.

- *Be mindful of evidence.* This is the hardest guideline to follow, for professionals often differ as to what they count as meaningful evidence. Our own perspective is that authors who deliberately seek connections between student achievement and the practices they recommend deserve the credence of practitioners. It is a principle we follow ourselves, and you can be confident that the authors we invited to contribute to The Essential Library of PreK–2 Literacy meet this criterion.

- *Match titles with topics.* If your team members have responded to the checklist in Figure 2.1, you can quickly identify gaps in your library. To fill these gaps, you'll need to acquire new titles.

- *Make your own professional learning syllabus.* Since you can't read all the books you identify at once, make a reasonable calendar to guide your work. Ask your teammates how much time they want to read and how much time they want to discuss what they've read.

Identifying Books

In addition to the six books we have edited in this series, we encourage you to check the titles you have against the list we've compiled in Figure 2.4. For example, let's assume that a team has collectively rated read-alouds as an area for which their knowledge of effective practice is moderate or limited. Let's also assume they have no resources for study. The book by Beauchat, Blamey, and Philippakos would be a good fit. In addition, some of the books listed contain chapters on this topic, such as *Promoting Early Reading* (McKenna, Walpole, & Conradi, 2010). Because of limited space, however, we have not provided the table of contents for the books listed. However, you can find it in many nonfiction books by clicking on *Amazon. com's* "Look Inside" feature.

Keep in mind that all of the topics listed in Figure 2.1 are addressed by the authors of the books in The Essential Library of PreK–2 Literacy. These authors

The Essential Library of PreK–2 Literacy

Coker, D. L., Jr., & Ritchey, K. D. (2015). *Teaching beginning writers.* New York: Guilford Press.

Hayes, L., & Flanigan, K. (2014). *Developing word recognition.* New York: Guilford Press.

Kuhn, M. R., & Levy, L. (2015). *Developing fluent readers: Teaching fluency as a foundational skill.* New York: Guilford Press.

Mesmer, H. A. E., Mesmer, E., & Jones, J. (2014). *Reading intervention in the primary grades: A common-sense guide to RTI.* New York: Guilford Press.

Silverman, R. D., & Hartranft, A. M. (2015). *Developing vocabulary and oral language in young children.* New York: Guilford Press.

Stahl, K. A. D., & Garcia, G. E. (2015). *Developing reading comprehension: Effective instruction for all students in PreK–2.* New York: Guilford Press.

Differentiated Instruction

Walpole, S., & McKenna, M. C. (2009). *How to plan differentiated reading instruction: Resources for grades K–3.* New York: Guilford Press.

Read-Alouds

Beauchat, K. A., Blamey, K. L., & Philippakos, Z. A. (2012). *Effective read-alouds for early literacy: A teacher's guide for PreK–1.* New York: Guilford Press.

Justice, L. M., & Sofka, A. E. (2010). *Engaging children with print: Building early literacy skills through quality read-alouds.* New York: Guilford Press.

Preschool

Beauchat, K. A., Blamey, K. L., & Walpole, S. (2010). *The building blocks of preschool success.* New York: Guilford Press.

McKenna, M. C., Walpole, S., & Conradi, K. (Eds.). (2010). *Promoting early reading: Research, resources, and best practices.* New York: Guilford Press.

Word Recognition and Spelling

Bear, D. R., Invernizzi, M., Templeton, S., & Johnston, F. (2015). *Words their way: Word study for phonics, vocabulary, and spelling instruction* (6th ed.). Upper Saddle River, NJ: Pearson.

Ganske, K. (2013). *Word journeys: Assessment-guided phonics, spelling, and vocabulary instruction* (2nd ed.). New York: Guilford Press.

O'Connor, R. E. (2014). *Teaching word recognition: Effective strategies for students with learning difficulties* (2nd ed.). New York: Guilford Press.

Fluency

Opitz, M. F., & Rasinski, T. V. (2008). *Good-bye round robin: 25 effective oral reading strategies* (updated ed.). Portsmouth, NH: Heinemann.

Standards

Morrow, L. M., Shanahan, T., & Wixson, K. K. (Eds.). (2013). *Teaching with the Common Core State Standards for English language arts: PreK–2.* New York: Guilford Press.

Neuman, S. B., & Gambrell, L. B. (Eds.). (2013). *Quality reading instruction in the age of Common Core Standards.* Newark, DE: International Reading Association.

Reutzel, D. R., & Cooter, R. B. (2015). *Strategies for reading assessment and instruction in an era of Common Core Standards: Helping every child succeed* (5th ed.). Upper Saddle River, NJ: Pearson.

(continued)

FIGURE 2.4. Recommended books for professional growth.

Grammar

Killgallon, D., & Killgallon, J. (2000). *Sentence composing for elementary school.* Portsmouth, NH: Heinemann.

Killgallon, D., & Killgallon, J. (2008). *Story grammar for elementary school: A sentence composing approach.* Portsmouth, NH: Heinemann.

Vocabulary

Beck, I. L., McKeown, M. G., & Kucan, L. (2013). *Bringing words to life: Robust vocabulary instruction* (2nd ed.). New York: Guilford Press.

Beck, I. L., McKeown, M. G., & Kucan, L. (2008). *Creating robust vocabulary: Frequently asked questions and extended examples.* New York: Guilford Press.

Kame'enui, E. J., & Baumann, J. F. (Eds.). (2012). *Vocabulary instruction: Research to practice* (2nd ed.). New York: Guilford Press.

Writing

Harris, K., Graham, S., Mason, L., & Friedlander, B. (2013). *Powerful writing strategies for all students.* Baltimore: Brookes.

Graham, S., MacArthur, C. A., & Fitzgerald, J. (Eds.). (2013). *Best practices in writing instruction* (2nd ed.). New York: Guilford Press.

Assessment and Intervention

McKenna, M. C., & Stahl, K. A. D. (2015). *Assessment for reading instruction* (3rd ed.). New York: Guilford Press.

O'Connor, R. E., & Vadasy, P. F. (Eds.). (2011). *Handbook of reading interventions.* New York: Guilford Press.

Stahl, K. A. D., & McKenna, M. C. (2013). *Reading assessment in an RTI framework.* New York: Guilford Press.

Research Summaries

Dickinson, D. K., & Neuman, S. B. (Eds.). (2006). *Handbook of early literacy research* (Vol. 2). New York: Guilford Press.

MacArthur, C. A., Graham, S., & Fitzgerald, J. (Eds.). (2016). *Handbook of writing research* (2nd ed.). New York: Guilford Press.

Neuman, S. B., & Dickinson, D. K. (Eds.). (2002). *Handbook of early literacy research* (Vol. 1). New York: Guilford Press.

Neuman, S. B., & Dickinson, D. K. (Eds.). (2011). *Handbook of early literacy research* (Vol. 3). New York: Guilford Press.

Reutzel, D. R. (Ed.). (2013). *Handbook of research-based practice in early education.* New York: Guilford Press.

FIGURE 2.4. *(continued)*

would be the first to caution you, however, that their books are not intended to be a definitive treatment of the topics. Other books can often complement these six books in productive ways.

Getting Beyond the Bookshelf: Online Sources

In an increasingly digital world, the idea of assembling a library of print books may strike you as a bit old school (literally). We find, however, that there are lots of growing pains associated with going digital. During the transition, many if not most teachers find it convenient to use print resources at least to some extent. Nevertheless, texts in digital form are here to stay, and we recommend a number of possibilities for building them into your professional learning library.

* *Consider e-books.* Many of the books listed in Figure 2.4 are available in digital form. For example, all of the books in The Essential Library are available for both the Kindle and the Nook. Going digital may make a book more difficult to share, however, and in some cases the price of the digital version is higher because of production costs.

* *Create PDFs.* Key chapters can be scanned into PDF form. They can then be shared, either by transferring them directly from teacher to teacher or by storing them in a dropbox or learning management system (LMS). (Check with your IT office for guidance concerning district and copyright policy.)

* *Locate PDFs.* Many PDFs are available free as a function of government agencies and nonprofit organizations. Important sources include the Carnegie Corporation, the U.S. Department of Education, the Center on Instruction, and others. We have assembled in Figure 2.5 a "starter set" of PDFs that we think should be in any primary library. Note in particular the *sources* of the PDFs. There are lots more where these came from!

* *Think modular.* Online modules can provide an engaging interactive framework for learning content. Our own website, *www.comprehensivereadingsolutions.com*, is one example. It contains free, open-access modules addressing all of the topics addressed in The Essential Library as well as many others. You can use the modules to complement and extend the content of the books. By providing podcasts and videos as well as text, the modules make it possible for topics to come alive and, we think, to better appreciate classroom implementation of new approaches. On the homepage you first select the desired age range: Birth–PreK or Grades K–5. You then choose a module by topic and work through it individually or with colleagues. At this writing, the modules have been accessed by teachers in every state and over 170 countries worldwide. Key features of the modules are listed in Figure 2.6.

Trivette, C. M, Simkus, A., Dunst, C. J., & Hamby, D. W. (2012). Repeated book reading and preschoolers' early literacy development. *CELLreviews, 5*(5), 1–13. Available at: *http://earlyliteracylearning.org/cellreviews/cellreviews_5_n5.pdf.*

More Practice Guides from the Center for Early Literacy Learning: *http://earlyliteracylearning. org/pgpracts.php*

What Works Clearinghouse. (2010). *Improving reading comprehension in kindergarten through 3rd grade: Practice guide.* Washington, DC: Institute of Education Sciences, U.S. Department of Education. Available at: *http://ies.ed.gov/ncee/wwc/PracticeGuide.aspx?sid=14.*

More Practice Guides from WWC: *http://ies.ed.gov/ncee/wwc/Publications_Reviews.aspx?f= All%20Publication%20and%20Product%20Types,3;#pubsearch*

Center on Instruction. (2007). *Extensive reading interventions in grades K–3: From research to practice.* Portsmouth, NH: RMC Research Corp., Center on Instruction. Available at: *www.centeroninstruction.org/files/Extensive%20Reading%20interventions.pdf.*

More Practice Guides from COI: *www.centeroninstruction.org/topic.cfm?s=1&k=L&c=18*

National Early Literacy Panel. (2008). *Developing early literacy: Report of the National Early Literacy Panel.* Washington, DC: National Institute for Literacy. Available at: *http://lincs.ed.gov/publications/pdf/NELPReport09.pdf.*

FIGURE 2.5. Selected free PDFs and key sources.

- Anonymous use without registering, logging in, or accepting cookies
- Pre- and post-self-assessments
- Videos and podcasts integrated with text
- Free materials and resources for download
- Hover effects
- Built-in activities
- Suggestions for group study
- Complete references

FIGURE 2.6. Key features of modules at *www.comprehensivereadingsolutions.com.*

Using Your Library

Think of your professional library as a work in progress. There will always be new books to add, new online resources to locate and explore. The important thing is not to wait until you have compiled an extensive library before taking action. As soon as a few key sources have been identified, it is time to learn!

We have already suggested that you employ a two-part system once a professional resource has been selected. The first part is individual study once a time-frame has been established. The second is learning together as a team.

Forming Study Teams

There are several ways to form an effective team, and the best way will depend on your topic and purpose:

• *Grade-level team.* A team comprising teachers at the same grade level has obvious advantages. Its members share many of the same concerns, and topics can be selected that are central to effective instruction at a particular grade (fluency at grade 2, for example). Moreover, they can observe and conference with one another rather easily.

• *RTI team.* Teachers charged with working within a response-to-intervention (RTI) framework share many professional learning interests. An RTI team might consist of a reading specialist, a special educator, and grade-level chairs. Together they can learn how to better coordinate their efforts.

• *Cross-grade team.* Grade-level representatives, including PreK, can function as a team where topics involve vertical articulation of the curriculum. For example, careful study of the standards would be an excellent instructional focus for such a team.

As these examples suggest, it is quite possible for a teacher to be a part of more than a single team. As long as the demands are reasonable, that can be a broadening experience.

Making a Personal Development Plan

Teamwork may be the lifeblood of professional learning, but there is room for an individual plan as well. When you compare the results of the self-survey with your teammates, you may very well find areas in which you judge your own knowledge to be limited compared with that of the others. For example, a novice teacher or one who has just been transferred to an unfamiliar grade level is likely to feel underprepared in some areas.

As long as you are sufficiently motivated, there is no reason why you can't pursue a professional learning agenda on your own. From the books, modules, and other resources we have identified in this chapter, you can craft a plan that is tailored to your own needs. And because of the inevitable overlap across the areas of early literacy development, your individual work will undoubtedly reinforce the learning you undertake as part of the team. So why wait?

Summary

We view ongoing professional learning as the heart of teaching as a profession. In this chapter, we have given you suggestions of evidence-based print and digital resources that we have actually read and used with teachers. We urge you to take charge of your own learning rather than waiting for your district to design it. Your own reading, plus your collaboration with colleagues, can be a continuing source of improvement in knowledge of both the science and the craft of teaching and learning in the early grades.

CHAPTER 3

Understanding Your Curriculum

- How do standards translate into methods and materials?
- What do the standards prescribe concerning methods and materials?
- How can you tell if the materials you are using are consistent with the standards?
- How can you judge whether the instructional approaches you employ are likely to help students meet the standards?
- What role should technology play in standards-based early literacy classrooms?

Examining the CCSS

The new standards have occasioned a flurry of dialogue, reflection, consternation, and policy debate. We find the exchanges generally welcome and the questions they raise in the best interest of young children. How will the standards be assessed? How can we implement them effectively? What happens if we fail? It's likely you've participated in the conversation. If so, you're aware of the complexity of the issues involved and of the need to consider them clearly.

We support the standards, as do many of the researchers we respect. We agree, for example, with Susan Neuman and Linda Gambrell (2013), who have written that the standards "represent a high bar but one that we should reach for in the field of reading and literacy learning for students across the grade levels" (p. 1).

McLaughlin and Overturf (2012) go further, noting that "implementing the Common Core State Standards is not an easy task, but it is an urgent one" (p. 164).

In this chapter, we examine a small part of the CCSS (NGA & CCSSO, 2010) Namely, we're concerned only with ELA in kindergarten, first grade, and second grade. (Though the Standards do not extend below kindergarten, preschool teachers must examine the kindergarten expectations for which they are preparing their students.)

We begin with the overarching question of how the Standards are to be implemented. To address this question, we'll need to be clear about the terms we use. Our work in schools has convinced us that some confusion persists about several key terms, and in particular the distinction between a set of standards and a curriculum. In Figure 3.1, we offer a working definition of each.

As you can see, standards are distinct from a curriculum. Standards come first and must be articulated into curricular objectives. When the objectives are achieved, the standard is met. A similar distinction is needed where materials are concerned. Materials can only be said to be "aligned" with the CCSS when they are part of a curriculum that is aligned. The Common Core does not prescribe materials or instructional methods:

> The Standards define what all students are expected to know and be able to do, not how teachers should teach. For instance, the use of play with young children is not specified by the Standards, but it is welcome as a valuable activity in its own right and as a way to help students meet the expectations in this document. (NGA & CCSSO, 2010, p. 6)

It is up to teachers to ensure that the materials they use and the methods they employ are likely to move their students toward accomplishing the Standards. Figure 3.2 summarizes the process.

What Do the Standards Say?

The CCSS for the ELA are more than a simple list. They consist of anchor standards, which cut across grade levels, and grade-level standards, which express the expectations related to each of the anchor standards at each grade. For example, Anchor Standard 1 for reading is:

Standards	Curriculum
End-of-year expectations for literacy achievement	A sequence of measurable objectives designed to meet one or more standards

FIGURE 3.1. Key distinction between standards and a curriculum.

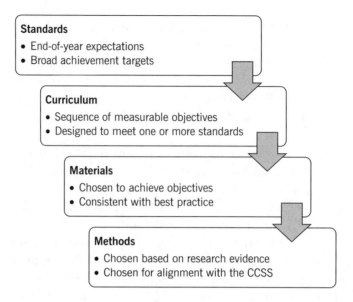

FIGURE 3.2. How standards should trickle down to materials.

> Read closely to determine what the text says explicitly and to make logical inferences from it; cite specific textual evidence when writing or speaking to support conclusions drawn from the text. (NGA & CCSSO, 2010, p. 10)

At second grade, the corresponding standard for reading literature is:

> Ask and answer such questions as who, what, where, when, why, and how to demonstrate understanding of key details in a text. (NGA & CCSSO, 2010, p. 10)

The ELA standards are classified in four broad categories—reading, writing, speaking and listening, and language—and reading is partitioned into three subareas: literature, informational text, and foundational skills.

Confused? It isn't really as complicated as it seems, and a bit of study will soon make the framework familiar. Figure 1.2 is one way to see how the standards are organized, and Figure 3.3 can help further. It gives the overall organization of the ELA standards.

The anchor standards take on more specific form in the standards at each grade level. The anchor standards for reading appear in Figure 3.4.

Note that they pertain to all types of reading, including the reading of literature and informational texts. But at every grade level there are separate reading standards for these two kinds of reading. Note too that the 10 anchor standards fall into four categories. These categories are repeated at each grade level. Figure 3.5 presents the standards for reading literature at kindergarten, first grade, and

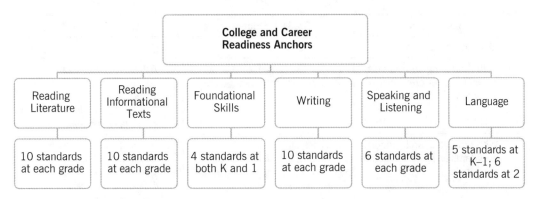

FIGURE 3.3. Overall organization of the CCSS for ELA.

Key Ideas and Details

1. Read closely to determine what the text says explicitly and to make logical inferences from it; cite specific textual evidence when writing or speaking to support conclusions drawn from the text.
2. Determine central ideas or themes of a text and analyze their development; summarize the key supporting details and ideas.
3. Analyze how and why individuals, events, and ideas develop and interact over the course of a text.

Craft and Structure

4. Interpret words and phrases as they are used in a text, including determining technical, connotative, and figurative meanings, and analyze how specific word choices shape meaning or tone.
5. Analyze the structure of texts, including how specific sentences, paragraphs, and larger portions of the text (e.g., a section, chapter, scene, or stanza) relate to each other and the whole.
6. Assess how point of view or purpose shapes the content and style of a text.

Integration of Knowledge and Ideas

7. Integrate and evaluate content presented in diverse media and formats, including visually and quantitatively, as well as in words.
8. Delineate and evaluate the argument and specific claims in a text, including the validity of the reasoning as well as the relevance and sufficiency of the evidence.
9. Analyze how two or more texts address similar themes or topics in order to build knowledge or to compare the approaches the authors take.

Range of Reading and Level of Text Complexity

10. Read and comprehend complex literary and informational texts independently and proficiently.

FIGURE 3.4. CCSS anchor standards in reading. From National Governors Association Center for Best Practices and Council of Chief State School Officers (2010). Copyright 2010 by the National Governors Association Center for Best Practices and Council of Chief State School Officers. All rights reserved.

Kindergartners	Grade 1 Students	Grade 2 Students
Key Ideas and Details		
1. With prompting and support, ask and answer questions about key details in a text.	1. Ask and answer questions about key details in a text.	1. Ask and answer such questions as *who*, *what*, *where*, *when*, *why*, and *how* to demonstrate understanding of key details in a text.
2. With prompting and support, retell familiar stories, including key details.	2. Retell stories, including key details, and demonstrate understanding of their central message or lesson.	2. Recount stories, including fables and folktales from diverse cultures, and determine their central message, lesson, or moral.
3. With prompting and support, identify characters, settings, and major events in a story.	3. Describe characters, settings, and major events in a story, using key details.	3. Describe how characters in a story respond to major events and challenges.
Craft and Structure		
4. Ask and answer questions about unknown words in a text.	4. Identify words and phrases in stories or poems that suggest feelings or appeal to the senses.	4. Describe how words and phrases (e.g., regular beats, alliteration, rhymes, repeated lines) supply rhythm, and meaning in a story, poem, or song.
5. Recognize common types of texts (e.g., storybooks, poems).	5. Explain major differences between books that tell stories and books that give information, drawing on a wide reading of a range of text types.	5. Describe how the overall structure of a story, including describing how the beginning introduces the story and the ending concludes the action.
6. With prompting and support, name the author and illustrator of a story and define the role of each in telling the story.	6. Identify who is telling the story at various points in a text.	6. Acknowledge differences in the points of view of characters, including by speaking in a different voice for each character when reading dialogue aloud.
Integration of Knowledge and Ideas		
7. With prompting and support, describe the relationship between illustrations and the story in which they appear (e.g., what moment in a story an illustration depicts).	7. Use illustrations and details in a story to describe its characters, setting, or events.	7. Use information gained from the illustrations and words in a print or digital text to demonstrate understanding of its characters, setting, or plot.

(continued)

FIGURE 3.5. CCSS reading literature standards for K–2. From National Governors Association Center for Best Practices, Council of Chief State School Officers (2010). Copyright 2010 by the National Governors Association Center for Best Practices and Council of Chief State School Officers. All rights reserved.

Kindergartners	Grade 1 Students	Grade 2 Students
8. (Not applicable to literature)	8. (Not applicable to literature)	8. (Not applicable to literature)
9. With prompting and support, compare and contrast the adventures and experiences of characters in familiar stories.	9. Compare and contrast the adventures and experiences of characters in stories.	9. Compare and contrast two or more versions of the same story (e.g., Cinderella stories) by different authors or from different cultures.
Range of Reading and Level of Text Complexity		
10. Actively engage in group reading activities with purpose and understanding.	10. With prompting and support, read prose and poetry of appropriate complexity for grade 1.	10. By the end of the year, read and comprehend literature, including stories and poetry, in the grades 2–3 text complexity band proficiently, with scaffolding as needed at the high end of the range.

FIGURE 3.5. *(continued)*

second grade. Choose any row and read across from left to right. You'll notice that the same standard is worded in more sophisticated language as you move from grade to grade. In other words, more is expected of students with respect to the anchor standard.

Dorothy Strickland has summarized the logic of revisiting the same anchor standard in more and more advanced contexts. She compares it with an upward spiral: "Instruction should address grade-specific standards in tandem with the broader goals of eventual college and career readiness. This concept, sometimes referred to as *spiraling*, involves similar standards expressed with increasing complexity from grade to grade" (2013, p. 16).

Foundational skills represent a third component of the reading standards. They differ from the literature and informational text standards in three important ways. First, there are no anchor standards. Second, because the standards follow the established developmental sequence, some standards are relevant only to certain grades. Figure 3.6 provides a quick overview of which standards are relevant to each grade. Finally, the standards are delineated into lettered elements, which really amount to objectives. This makes sense because the foundational skills are mostly constrained in nature. That is, once they're acquired, the student moves on to new skills rather than spiraling to more sophisticated versions of the same skill.

Examining the standards carefully is critically important if you are to plan and provide instruction that is likely to help your students meet them. Unless you're familiar with what the standards require, you'll be unable to think about them in curricular terms or to choose methods and materials that are likely to be most appropriate. The ELA document itself would make an excellent book study for a grade-level or cross-grade team.

	Kindergarten	First Grade	Second Grade
Print Concepts	✓	✓	
Phonological Awareness	✓	✓	
Phonics and Word Recognition	✓	✓	✓
Fluency	(Minimal)	✓	✓

FIGURE 3.6. Foundational skills addressed in the primary grades.

We further suggest that you look across grade levels, examining the full range of elementary standards from kindergarten through fifth grade in each of the four ELA categories. Doing so will acquaint you with the upward progress toward the end goal of college and career readiness, a goal that propelled the development of the Common Core to begin with. In other words, gaining some perspective on where the standards direct the efforts of teachers at each grade will give you an improved sense of how your own practice fits into the bigger picture. McLaughlin and Overturf (2012) have suggested the following activity: "Within each category, read vertically within each grade level, from kindergarten through grade 5, to gain a general understanding of how the standards are structured and what the more specific expectations are" (p. 155).

We have paid special attention to Anchor Standard 10, Range of Reading and Level of Text Complexity. It does not really kick in until grade 2, but that means that kindergarten and grade 1 have to ensure that students are ready for those materials when they start grade 2. Beginning at grade 2, this standard is expressed with reference to Lexiles in the Appendix of the standards document. Lexiles are quantitative measures of text difficulty. Students in grades 2 and 3 should be reading texts in the 450–790 range. We use those definitions of text complexity to evaluate materials for grade 2 and to build curriculum for grades K and 1; in short, very strong foundational skills achievement is required to make that entry text level for second grade. Stahl and García (2015) in this series offer a more extensive discussion of the Lexile framework.

Taking Stock of Your Materials

Once you've familiarized yourself with what the standards require, you can move to curriculum and materials. We're all familiar with sticker shock. When you see that the sticker price of a new car or some other large purchase is far higher than you'd thought, you're taken aback. But there is another kind of sticker shock. Many of the commercial reading materials now on the market carry stickers claiming that the program is the "Common Core Edition" or that it is "Common Core

Aligned." We don't claim to have reviewed every reading program now available, but in our experience such claims are suspect.

To judge the extent to which a program is actually consistent with the CCSS, it's necessary to compare it with the essential requirements of the Standards. With respect to the program or curriculum map you're presently using, or one you're considering adopting, ask yourself the following questions.

1. *Are the texts included written within the grade-level Lexile bands determined by the Standards?* This question represents the single most important (and controversial) issue in the Common Core. Engaging students at every grade in more challenging texts, both for reading and listening, means that business-as-usual approaches are often inadequate. You can easily spot check the Lexile levels of selections by locating them in the open-access database at *Lexile.com*. If you're curious about a particular selection and can't locate it, you can type a sample and upload it using the Lexile Analyzer tool. (See Stahl and García, 2015, in The Essential Library of PreK–2 Literacy series for a thorough discussion of text selection.)

2. *Do the selections include genres specified in the Standards?* Although the CCSS do not include every genre that may be important, the Standards often list genres, if only as examples. Whenever genres are specified, an aligned program should include them. For example, a second-grade program should include fables and folktales from various cultures (see Figure 3.5, Standard 2).

3. *Is there a balance of literature and informational selections?* In the primary grades, balance means 50–50. "One common misconception is that the reading standards leave no room for literary texts," Halladay and Duke have observed (2013, p. 44). "Through grade 4," they point out, "the standards call for half of all reading time to be devoted to literary text." Remember that the *number* of selections is not the important factor. It's the *length* of the selections that matters.

4. *Does the program address all 10 standards in each of the literacy domains included?* Remember that there are four domains and that reading is divided into three sections. In fairness, a particular program may not be comprehensive, and if this is the case, it should be evaluated with respect to the domains it does address. The grade-level Standards should be evaluated based on the extent to which the program specifically explains how each Standard is addressed. This explanation may appear only in the teacher's edition (TE).

5. *Are the Standards clearly associated with lesson plans?* The TE should spell out how the Standards are addressed in each lesson. For example, if a first-grade plan indicates that a teacher should prompt children to describe the setting of a story, the plan should indicate that doing so reflects one standard for reading literature (see Figure 3.5, Standard 3). Failure to provide explicit connections with the CCSS doesn't necessarily mean that a program is misaligned, of course, but it

would behoove a user to make a judgment. And that would require a great deal of time. (Note that this issue is not the same as the one we raised in the previous question. Not every standard applies to every lesson. The overall program should address them all, and each lesson should specify which standards are relevant.)

6. *Are the four foundational dimensions ordered appropriately?* The CCSS limits print concepts and phonological awareness to kindergarten and first grade. This is not to say that problems in these areas cannot occur in later grades, but they are rare and typically warrant intensive intervention. A program that includes these dimensions as part of the grade-level curriculum at second grade risks diverting time away from more advanced skills.

7. *Are foundational skills addressed systematically?* This question is relatively easy to answer because the foundational standards are broken down into specific skills (designated with letters). You can determine how well they map onto the scope and sequence of the program.

Taking Stock of Your Methods

The Common Core does not prescribe specific instructional approaches. That job is left to others. Where to find sources that describe such approaches is a fair question. Certainly the principle guiding your search must be to make sure that the approaches are aligned with the Standards and that they are evidence based. This is where The Essential Library of PreK-2 Literacy can be especially useful. In fact, we've come to view it as a place for one-stop shopping in order to meet the challenges of the Common Core!

The contributing authors to this series have written with this principle in mind. For example, Stahl and García (2015) describe approaches to questioning and writing to prompts that are consistent with the standards. Coker and Ritchey (2015) present a number of well-aligned approaches to composition and handwriting. Silverman and Hartranft (2015) describe numerous standards-based methods of fostering language and vocabulary development. Hayes and Flanigan (2014) detail well-researched approaches to teaching word recognition, and Kuhn and Levy (2015) discuss fluency approaches that are likely to produce the growth expected by the new standards.

Thinking about the Role of Technology

The CCSS do not contain a strand devoted to technology. At first, this might strike you as a glaring omission. However, the framers of the CCSS chose to integrate technology wherever appropriate rather than isolating its use. For example, in

Figure 3.5 you'll note that reading literature Standard 7 at grade 2 speaks to information gained "from illustrations and words in a print *or digital* text" (emphasis added). So the expectation is clear, and while technology use is not highlighted in a separate category, it permeates all four ELA areas.

From the beginning of the digital age, many primary teachers have resisted this charge (Turbill & Murray, 2006). They argue that only "real" books, those with physical form, should be used. If you share this bias, we urge you to consider the world you are preparing your students to enter. Adherence to it may also further disadvantage those children who lack access to technology at home. As Wohlwend (2010) has noted, "when this ideal becomes a policy or curricular stance, it further distances our youngest learners from access to digital technologies that make up modern literacies" (p. 146).

The first step in addressing the standards is to note where technology use is explicitly included. Figure 3.7, compiled by McKenna, Conradi, Young, and Jang (2013), pinpoints the standards at kindergarten, first grade, and second grade. As always, preschool educators should note the kindergarten applications.

Summary

The CCSS for ELA are, with the exception of foundational skills, expressed as 10 overarching anchor standards in each dimension of literacy. The anchor standards are then stated in more specific terms at each grade level. Implementation requires that the standards next be expressed as specific curricular objectives, and that materials and methods then be chosen to help students achieve those objectives.

Full implementation of the Common Core is challenging because the new standards present teachers in the primary grades with the need to make a number of changes in traditional practice. These include the use of more challenging texts, a balance of literature and informational texts, a systematic approach to foundational skills, and early integration of technology. Although primary teachers have often resisted the use of technology, the standards are clear.

Area	Standard	Kindergarten	Grade 1	Grade 2
Literature	7			Use information gained from the illustrations and words in a print or digital text to demonstrate understanding of its characters, setting, or plot.
Informational Text	5		Know and use various text features (e.g., headings, tables of contents, glossaries, electronic menus, icons) to locate key facts or information in a text.	Know and use various text features (e.g., captions, bold print, subheadings, glossaries, indexes, electronic menus, icons) to locate key facts or information in a text efficiently.
Writing	6	With guidance and support from adults, explore a variety of digital tools to produce and publish writing, including in collaboration with peers.	With guidance and support from adults, use a variety of digital tools to produce and publish writing, including in collaboration with peers.	With guidance and support from adults, use a variety of digital tools to produce and publish writing, including in collaboration with peers.
Speaking and Listening	2	Confirm understanding of a text read-aloud or information presented orally or through other media by asking and answering questions about key details and requesting clarification if something is not understood.	Ask and answer questions about key details in a text read-aloud or information presented orally or through other media.	Recount or describe key ideas or details from a text read-aloud or information presented orally or through other media.
	5	Add drawings or other visual displays to descriptions as desired to provide additional detail.	Add drawings or other visual displays to descriptions when appropriate to clarify ideas, thoughts, and feelings.	Create audio recordings of stories or poems; add drawings or other visual displays to stories or recounts of experiences when appropriate to clarify ideas, thoughts, and feelings.
Language	4			Determine or clarify the meaning of unknown and multiple-meaning words and phrases based on *grade 2 reading and content*, choosing flexibly from an array of strategies: Use glossaries and beginning dictionaries, both print and digital, to determine or clarify the meaning of words and phrases.

FIGURE 3.7. Technology use in the K–2 CCSS for ELA. From National Governors Association Center for Best Practices and Council of Chief State School Officers (2010). Copyright 2010 by the National Governors Association Center for Best Practices and Council of Chief State School Officers. All rights reserved.

CHAPTER 4
• • • • • • • • • •

Creating an Assessment Plan

GUIDING QUESTIONS

• What types of literacy assessments are useful in the primary grades?
• How can assessments best be used to identify instructional needs?
• How do assessment strategies differ between the earlier and later primary grades?
• How should assessments work in a response to intervention system?
• How can assessments help you reflect on your teaching?

Think back to your last physical. Your doctor ran a number of tests to determine the state of your health, tests that varied considerably in the kinds of information they yielded. They ranged from a simple reflex hammer to a complex chemical analysis of your blood. Together, they presented the doctor with a broad profile of where you stood. If all the results were within normal limits, you got a "clean bill of health." If, however, some of the tests yielded problematic findings, your doctor took steps to address them, perhaps through recommendations or prescriptions and perhaps by ordering additional tests. In any case, the doctor likely planned to revisit the findings in order to monitor the situation over time.

This well-established model of medical practice has been adapted for use in education, and it works well in certain areas. Given a small set of appropriate tests, teachers can identify literacy needs, provide instruction to meet those needs, and gauge the success of that instruction. In this chapter, we present an overview of a simple system of assessment designed to help you systematically address student needs and provide you with the information needed to reflect meaningfully on your teaching.

Understanding the Purposes of Assessment

There is an old saying that the best doctors have lots of patients and the best teachers have lots of patience. True enough, but step into a physician's shoes for a moment and think of your students as "patients." Not because they are sick. It may help you to view your mission broadly, the way modern doctors do, to include promoting "wellness" in addition to healing the sick. A broad perspective means that every student is a patient and that even those who are making good progress bear attention.

In the role of teacher-as-physician, you need information to help you address several important questions:

- Which students are making acceptable progress in literacy growth?
- In which areas are some students struggling?
- How can you specifically address the needs of those who struggle?
- How can you determine whether your efforts are successful?
- If your efforts are unsuccessful, how should you plan next steps?

Using a surprisingly small set of reliable assessments, you can answer these questions as a routine part of your practice as a teacher. Figure 4.1 presents these questions as part of an overall decision-making system. As in medicine, the system applies to one dimension at a time.

Four Types of Assessments and What They Tell Us

Assessments designed to answer these questions are of three basic kinds.

1. *Screening assessments* can tell us whether there is a problem in a particular area. They are usually associated with benchmark scores, which aid in interpreting the results. Falling below the benchmark for a certain grade and time of year signals a potential problem. The information that screening assessments provide, however, is not specific enough to plan the instruction needed to address a problem once it's identified. A screening test that measures decoding proficiency, for example, could indicate a problem but would offer no guidance concerning how to address it. That's where diagnostic assessments come in.

2. *Diagnostic assessments* are fine-grained enough to permit you to plan targeted instruction. They are administered only as a follow-up to screening assessments. A phonics inventory, for example, might be given if a screening assessment in decoding indicated a problem in this area. We want to stress that diagnostic assessments can be informal in nature. They need not be highly technical instruments that require special training.

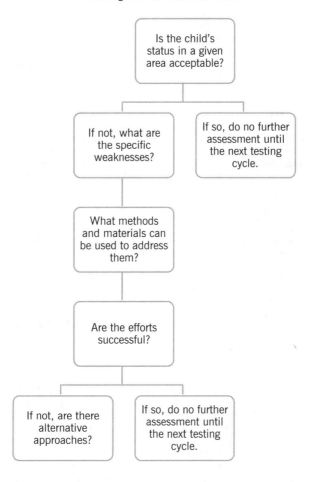

FIGURE 4.1. The logic of literacy assessment in the primary grades.

3. *Progress monitoring assessments* can tell you whether your efforts are bearing fruit or whether an alternative approach is called for. Once you've begun to provide targeted instruction, it's important to regularly gauge how well it's working. You'd never want to continue using approaches and materials that are getting the child nowhere. A progress monitoring assessment could simply be an alternate form of the screening assessment, but it is now given for a different purpose, that of determining whether or not to continue an intervention.

Let's revisit the assessment system, this time connecting the key questions with the types of assessments that can help us answer them. Figure 4.2 shows how the three types of assessments are coordinated within the overall decision-making system. Note that it's the screening assessment that propels the process. As contributing authors Mesmer, Mesmer, and Jones point out, "The meaning of the verb *to screen* is to separate, divide, or partition, and that is exactly what

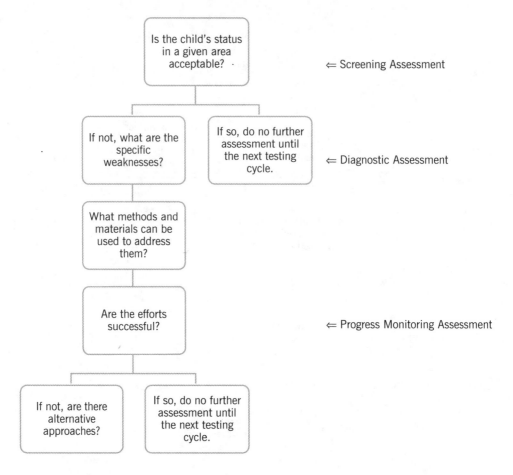

FIGURE 4.2. Types of assessments used to meet instructional needs.

screening measures do" (2014, p. 9). It is also the reason our decision tree branches after the screening test is given. We are partitioning the students in our class into two categories.

There is a fourth type of assessment as well, but it does not fit within the decision-making system. This is the outcome assessment, typically administered at the end of the school year. Outcome measures are often high stakes in nature, and an example is a group-administered, state-adopted end-of-year achievement test. However, screening tests can also serve as outcome measures, though they are not among the high-profile tests that tend to capture headlines. They can serve an important purpose nonetheless, by helping teachers, administrators and coaches collectively keep tabs on student progress in a range of areas. In this way, problems that may affect a particular grade level can get on the radar, and plans can be made to address them as a team. Figure 4.3 presents thumbnail descriptions of all four assessment types and the role of each.

Type	Description and Purpose
Screening	• Identifies problems in a particular area • Results are not specific enough to plan instruction
Diagnostic	• Given as a follow-up to a screening assessment when a problem is detected • Yields results specific enough for planning targeted instruction
Progress Monitoring	• Given to gauge the impact of targeted instruction • Often simply an alternate form of a screening assessment
Outcome	• Given to gauge the progress of groups • Could be the aggregated results of a screening test • Could be high stakes in nature

FIGURE 4.3. Four types of literacy assessments.

Using Assessments to Identify Needs

It is not necessary to apply the assessment model shown in Figure 4.2 to every dimension of reading. One reason is that the unconstrained dimensions, such as comprehension and vocabulary, can't be assessed in this way. To be clear, we are not at all suggesting that assessment in these areas is unimportant, and contributors to this series have suggested excellent approaches. Stahl and García (2015) present a number of effective ways to assess comprehension, and Silverman and Hartranft (2015) have done the same for vocabulary.

Fortunately, however, we don't need to assess vocabulary or comprehension to determine students' foundational skill needs. These can be identified quickly and systematically using the approach developed by Steven Stahl and his colleagues (Stahl, Kuhn, & Pickle, 1999). Their cognitive model of reading assessment amounts to asking a sequence of questions. These questions differ slightly depending on grade level.

Systematic Assessment Beginning in Late First Grade

Beginning in the middle of first grade, children should have acquired the proficiency needed to read easy texts fluently. To judge their oral reading fluency, predictive benchmarks are available, expressed as words correct per minute. Applying these benchmarks is the first question we ask in determining instructional needs in the area of foundational skills.

• *Is the child fluent in context?* If the answer is yes, further assessment is unnecessary, and we needn't continue our questioning.

• *Does the child have an adequate sight vocabulary?* Fluent oral reading requires more than a range of decoding skills. These skills lead naturally to the acquisition of words that a child can pronounce automatically, without having to consciously decode them. Listening to the child read orally can act as a way to informally screen this ability. Hesitating often at high-frequency words suggests that the child has acquired too few sight words. A diagnostic inventory of these words can be useful in selecting which words to teach.

• *Are there gaps in the child's decoding skills?* If the child is below the benchmark, it is important to determine whether gaps in decoding are to blame. The logic is compelling: It is not possible to apply skills quickly and automatically if you can't apply them slowly. An inventory of single-syllable decoding skills can help you answer this question. Before embarking on decoding instruction, however, it is important to ask one more question.

• *Has the child developed adequate phonological awareness?* The ability to recognize the sounds that make up spoken words is essential if the child is to associate those sounds with letters. A weakness in phonological awareness must be addressed directly if phonics instruction is to succeed. Here, an inventory of phonological awareness skills can be helpful.

Answering these questions in a systematic way can help you group children temporarily and flexibly until fluency benchmarks are reached. The process is captured in Figure 4.4.

Systematic Assessment in Kindergarten and Early First Grade

Throughout kindergarten and the first half of grade 1, teachers must work to develop the foundation of fluency. Because most children cannot yet read, their assessments do not focus directly on fluency but rather on the specific skills that are necessary to attain fluency. Determining instructional needs requires a slightly different set of questions. These are based on the curriculum in place, which means taking into account the sequence used to introduce skills. It does not make sense to assess skills that have not yet been taught, and the questions we ask are based on this assumption.

• *Is the child able to decode words requiring skills that have been introduced?* Assessments reflecting each new skill set can help monitor their attainment and identify the need for additional instruction in a timely manner. If the answer is yes, then proceeding to more sophisticated skills is appropriate. If not, then additional instruction will be required. However, a more basic question needs to be addressed first.

• *Does the child have adequate phonological awareness?* This step is the same throughout K–2. Without a foundation of phonological awareness, decoding

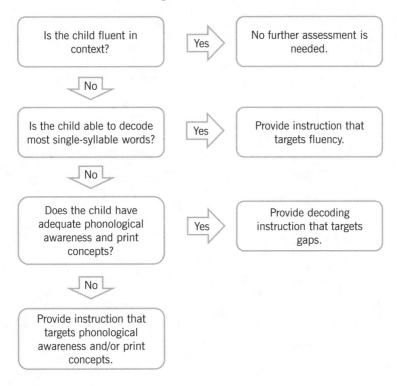

FIGURE 4.4. Assessing foundational skills from the middle of first grade.

instruction will not be fruitful. Children who wander off track when decoding instruction is conducted may do so for this reason.

You can address these questions systematically to shore up foundational gaps as quickly as possible. A great deal depends on it! We've captured the system in Figure 4.5.

Building an Assessment Toolkit

Answering the questions we've posed above requires the same kind of information, regardless of what grade you teach. The only way to get it is by conducting assessments. Doing so is not difficult. Nor is it technical or time consuming. A small assessment "toolkit" is all you need to provide instruction that targets a student's foundational skill needs. Because outcome assessments are not needed for this instruction, and because any screening assessment can double as a progress-monitoring test, you need only screening and diagnostic measures in the major areas of instruction. A starter set of these instruments appears in Figure 4.6. They

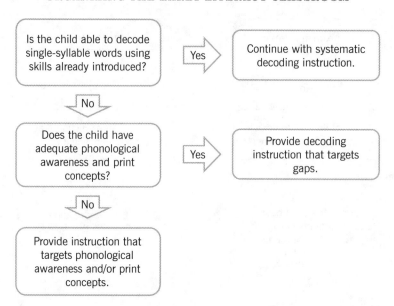

FIGURE 4.5. Assessing foundational skills in kindergarten through the middle of first grade.

Area of Literacy	Grades	Examples of Screening Assessments	Examples of Diagnostic Assessments
Phonological Awareness	K–1	DIBELS Next Phoneme Segmentation Fluency	Tests of Phonological Awareness (McKenna & Stahl, 2015)
Print Concepts	K–1	DIBELS Next Phoneme Segmentation Fluency	Alphabet Recognition Inventory Letter-Sound Inventory (McKenna & Stahl, 2015)
Decoding	K–1	DIBELS Next Nonsense Word Fluency	Informal Decoding Inventory (Walpole, McKenna, & Philippakos, 2011)
Sight Words	1–2	DIBELS Next Oral Reading Fluency Observation of oral reading	Sight Word Inventory (Fry, Dolch, etc.)
Oral Reading Fluency	1–2	DIBELS Next Oral Reading Fluency	See assessments of decoding and sight words above

FIGURE 4.6. An assessment toolkit.

can be used with either of the models we've described in Figures 4.4 and 4.5. The list is drawn from our previous recommendations (McKenna & Stahl, 2015; McKenna & Walpole, 2005; Walpole & McKenna, 2009).

Let's consider three examples of how the system works—one at kindergarten, one at first grade, and one at second grade. Though other patterns may arise, these are among the most typical.

Zoi, a kindergartner, scores well below the benchmark on a midyear screening test of nonsense word fluency. This test required her to decode unfamiliar consonant–vowel–consonant (CVC) words such as *zat* and *fum*. The middle of kindergarten is the first time this screening test is given, and Ms. Wilson, Zoi's teacher, wants to determine the cause of the problem. So far, her decoding instruction has involved letter names and sounds and the decoding of CVC words. Zoi's inability to decode such words at the benchmark level is cause for concern. The decision-making model in Figure 4.5 suggests that Ms. Wilson begin by considering whether there is a problem related to the underlying skills, including letter recognition, letter sounds, and phonological awareness. Because the screening battery also includes a test of phoneme segmentation fluency, Ms. Wilson is able to use the result to rule out a deficit in phonological awareness as the root of Zoi's difficulty. In the fall, she had administered both an alphabet recognition inventory and a letter-sound inventory, and she can also rule out deficits in these areas. This means that the solution to Zoi's problem may lie in additional instruction in CVC decoding. Ms. Wilson confirms this conclusion by administering the Short Vowels subtest of the Informal Decoding Inventory. This assessment is untimed and focuses on 10 real and 10 nonsense CVC words presented in isolation. Zoi scores below the established criterion. Ms. Wilson has now confirmed that Zoi possesses the prerequisite foundational skills necessary for CVC decoding and that the instruction she has received has not been successful. She therefore takes steps to provide additional instruction at a more intensive level.

Jake is a first grader who has scored below the benchmark on a screening test of oral reading fluency administered in January. This is the earliest it is possible to give this assessment. Jake's teacher, Mr. Bergen, interprets the results using the plan presented in Figure 4.4. This means that he cannot come to the simple conclusion that Jake needs more instruction in fluency. Mr. Bergen must first eliminate the possibility that there are more fundamental problems. Because the screening assessment battery also includes a test of nonsense word fluency (administered for the last time at the beginning of grade one), Mr. Bergen notes that Jake has scored above the benchmark. This result eliminates the need to look deeper, at phonological awareness and print concepts, because it is impossible to score well on a test of nonsense word fluency without these skill sets. Mr. Bergen next considers the possibility that Jake may lack some of the decoding skills he has attempted to teach. So far, these include CVC words, words containing consonant blends and digraphs, and words with *r*-controlled vowels. He administers the three subtests of the Informal Decoding Inventory corresponding to these skills, and Jake exceeds the criteria. He also gives an inventory of high-frequency words and determines that Jake is able to recognize many of them. Mr. Bergen has followed the assessment model in Figure 4.4, and he can reasonably conclude that Jake will be best served by instruction that focuses on fluency.

Kristin is a second grader who has scored below benchmark on the oral reading fluency screening test administered at midyear. Her teacher, Ms. Henderson, follows the decision model in Figure 4.4 and hopes to rule out more basic difficulties. Although the screening test of nonsense word fluency is no longer given in the middle of second grade, it was administered at the start of the year, and Ms. Henderson checks the results. Because Kristin scored at benchmark, Ms. Henderson can quickly rule out basic skill prerequisites, such as phonological awareness and letter sounds. However, she is unwilling to rule out decoding deficits based on a general screening given five months earlier. She therefore takes the time to administer the five single-syllable subtests of the Informal Decoding Inventory together with a sight word inventory. Kristin performs well on the decoding measures, but she has acquired an inadequate number of sight words. Ms. Henderson places her in a group that will receive fluency instruction coupled with targeted work with sight words.

Making the Most of the Assessments You Have

We encourage teachers in the primary grades to use a common set of assessments. This policy enables better communication among teachers, and it helps ensure continuity as students pass from grade to grade. The assessments listed in Figure 4.6 provide a good basis, though specific decisions will need to be made. For example, there are alternatives to the measures we've listed. Hayes and Flanigan (2014) in their book in The Essential Library present options for assessing word recognition. In any case, you will need a toolkit addresses all of the foundational skills primary students need to acquire.

Adding Assessments Where Needed

You may find that your existing assessments address most of the needs but that gaps will need to be filled. You may also discover that some of the assessments you currently administer do not fit into the assessment models we've described. In these cases, you must decide whether the assessments serve a useful purpose.

Also, the assessments we've listed can become part of your school's RTI system. But they are only a part. A comprehensive RTI system will require additional measures associated with intensive interventions. In identifying a comprehensive set of assessments to drive an effective RTI system, examine the recommendations made by Mesmer, Mesmer, and Jones (2014) in this series.

Finally, you will need to work with both your grade-level team and the teachers at adjacent grades in making these decisions. A literacy coach can be extremely useful in coordinating the process and establishing a data system. If your school has no coach, another teacher or an administrator will need to assume this responsibility.

Using Assessments to Measure Learning

Earlier in this chapter, we made the point that outcome measures are not suited to the purpose of planning day-to-day instruction. They can, however, help us gauge the impact of our instruction over periods of time and across grade levels. A frequent mistake is to consider high-stakes achievement tests as the only outcome measures worth considering. These are obviously important, but we can actually learn more from examining group changes in the screening assessments we primarily use as a first step in planning instruction.

Judging the Impact of Your Program

Consider any measure with benchmarks, administered at the beginning, middle, and end of the school year. We will use the DIBELS Next Oral Reading Fluency subtest to illustrate our point. When it is first administered in the middle of grade 1, teachers can, of course, use the results to propel the assessment process we have described in this chapter. But the results can also be used for other purposes. To begin with, the mean score for all first graders at midyear can be compared with the end-of-year mean. In addition, the proportion of children scoring above the benchmark, between the benchmark and the cut score, and below the cut score at midyear, can be compared with the proportion at each level at the end of the year. Figure 4.7 illustrates a simple approach to making such a comparison. Note that although the mean (in words correctly read per minute) may have risen, the percentage of children below the benchmark has increased considerably.

This is only one example of how screening measures can provide telling indicators of a program's strengths and weaknesses. By aggregating assessment results at the level of the teacher, the grade, and the school, we can gauge the effectiveness of our reading program, and we can determine points at which change is required.

Judging Your Students' Response to Intervention

Data from all four types of measures can be used in tandem to track individual students over time. Screening assessment and follow-up diagnostic assessments can become the basis of a system for determining which students have not responded to your intervention efforts. These students can be tracked through increasingly intensive interventions until special education becomes a consideration. It is beyond

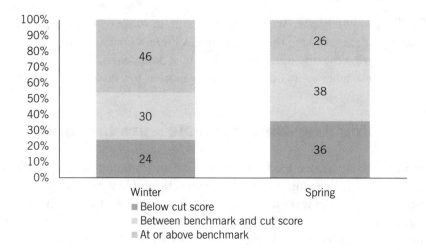

FIGURE 4.7. Distribution of students on the DIBELS Next Oral Reading Fluency subtest at two administrations.

the scope of this chapter to describe a response-to-intervention system in detail, but Mesmer, Mesmer, and Jones have done precisely that in their book in The Essential Library.

Using Assessments to Reflect on Your Teaching

When it comes to an individual classroom teacher, we tend to avoid the term *response to intervention*, preferring instead *response to instruction*. The reason is that even Tier One classroom instruction is worthy of measurement and reflection. It is true, of course, that the primary purpose of assessment is to inform instruction, but there is a second purpose as well, and it may be just as important. Assessments also reflect the effectiveness of our instruction, and the results can be powerful tools in seriously and sincerely reflecting on our practice. We encourage you to compile data for both purposes. The results can not only guide your efforts with students but can help you map a personal plan for professional growth. They can assist you in identifying your own strengths and weaknesses, and lead you in the direction of appropriate resources. And we can think of no better place to begin than with the books in The Essential Library of PreK–2 Literacy.

Summary

In this chapter, we have described four major types of assessments (screening, diagnostic, progress monitoring, and outcome) useful in guiding your instructional efforts. We outlined a step-by-step process for using these types of assessments in tandem to determine instructional needs and to plan appropriately. Our discussion was limited to the foundational skills because the less constrained skills, such as vocabulary and comprehension, do not lend themselves to diagnostic assessment.

We offered a slight distinction between how the diagnostic process should proceed for kindergarten and early first grade as opposed to the latter half of first grade and second grade. However, the logic in both cases is the same and proceeds along developmental lines, starting with more complex skills and proceeding where necessary to their underlying prerequisites.

We noted that only a small number of assessments are needed to propel the diagnostic process resulting in targeted instruction. This basic set of measures can form the basis of an RTI system, but additional measures would be needed for a comprehensive system that includes intensive interventions.

When the results are aggregated, they can assist in evaluating the impact of a reading program at the level of the classroom, the grade, and the school. At the classroom level, we suggested that these measures can gauge not only the learning of your students but the effectiveness of your teaching. We encouraged you to use the results for personal reflection in an effort to choose the most appropriate professional learning.

CHAPTER 5

· · · · · · · · · · ·

Linking Assessments
to Report Cards

- What are the purposes of a report card?
- What is a standards-based report card?
- What is "three-P grading"?
- How does a standards-based report card differ from a traditional card?
- What should a standards-based report card look like?
- How can you help parents understand a report card?
- How can a report card best serve exceptional and struggling learners?

As a classroom teacher, you may be wondering why we would include a chapter on report cards. After all, policies affecting the design and use of report cards are set by administrators, and it is the job of teachers to adhere to those policies. Although we don't dispute this notion, two reasons prompted us to include a discussion of report cards. The first is that you are part of a professional literacy community within your school. It is likely that you might at some point have a voice in altering the report card policy. You could, for example, serve on an assessment committee or offer informal suggestions to school leaders. The second reason is that by organizing the information you have in the manner we describe here, you will be in a better position to speak with parents about their children, even if you never send the information home.

In this chapter, we will address the purposes of a report card and offer an important distinction between the traditional version and a standards-based card.

We will also discuss the practice of providing parents with more than a single indicator so that they are able to get a broad perspective on how their children are doing.

Purposes of a Report Card

Several groups of stakeholders have a legitimate right to know how well students are performing. The most obvious group is parents, of course, but students can also benefit as can administrators and teachers. You might wonder what teachers stand to gain from the process, but completing a report card can be a very enlightening experience! Various types of data are drawn together and the result is a profile of each student, one that can provide insights you might otherwise not have had.

Muñoz and Guskey (2015) offer a useful distinction by breaking the process down into grading and reporting. Both are "foundational elements in every educational system. Grading represents teachers' evaluations—formative or summative—of students' performance. Reporting is how the results of those evaluations are communicated to students, parents, or others" (p. 64). Reporting serves the interests of all three sets of stakeholders. Although we have already argued that the process may assist teachers in making formative changes in their approaches to instruction, this is not the primary purpose of grading. Tomlinson and Moon (2013) express this idea well:

> Neither evidence nor common sense suggests that the grades are effective mechanisms for "fixing" student differences. The best-case scenario for grades is that they present students and parents with accurate and intelligible representations of development in a context where all efforts are aimed at moving students as far forward as possible from where they begin in a content area by addressing their varied readiness needs, interests, and approaches to learning. (pp. 137–138)

Rather, the kind of formative assessments that can signal the need to change, those that are designed to "provide feedback to modify the teaching and learning activities" (Black & Wiliam, 1998, p. 7), are more typically given *between* marking periods.

Moving from a Traditional to a Standards-Based Report Card

We suspect that you are already quite familiar with the traditional report card format, similar to the one represented in Figure 5.1 Each subject is assigned a letter grade intended to reflect overall achievement.

Student: *Pete*	Marking Period			
Subject	1	2	3	4
Reading	A			
Writing	B			
Math	A			
Science	C			
Social Studies	C			
Art	B			
P.E.	D			
Music	A			

FIGURE 5.1. Format of the traditional report card.

It's true that parents tend to be comfortable with this approach, mostly because it was used when they were students and they *think* they understand it (Guskey & Jung, 2013). But there are significant problems with the traditional report card. In the case of low grades, parents have little way of determining the nature of the problem or how to assist their child. In addition, teachers tend to vary in terms of how they distill an overall grade from a collection of test scores, daily work, and other information. Teachers often vary as to how much weight they assign to scores, and weighted scores are typically "combined in idiosyncratic ways" (Muñoz & Guskey, 2015, p. 64). Finally, letter grades can be hard to interpret. They can be assigned relative to the performance of other students, or they can reflect the degree to which a student has achieved learning outcomes. This is not to say that letter grades should be avoided, of course, but if they are used, their meaning must be clear. The key is "to ensure that grades, scores, or any other system can be effectively translated by parents" (Wiggins, 1994, p. 30).

Moving Away from a Single Grade

Unpacking an overall grade into its components makes it much easier for parents to understand how their children are performing. "Using a *single* grade with no clear and stable meaning to summarize all aspects of performance *is* a problem. We need more, not fewer grades; and more different *kinds* of grades and comments if the parent is to be informed" (Wiggins, 1994, p. 29, emphasis in original).

The difficulty is that there are several ways of producing more than a single grade. One approach is to separate achievement from other factors, such as behavior, effort, and attitude. Guskey and Bailey (2010) recommend that teachers assign grades in three broad areas: product, process, and progress. To do so, a teacher considers evidence—indicators—of each one. "After establishing indicators of product, process, and progress learning, teachers then assign separate grades to each indicator" (Muñoz & Guskey, 2015, p. 65). Tomlinson and Moon (2013) refer to this approach as "three-P grading," and they caution against the temptation to combine the three into a single grade. Doing so would defeat the purpose: *"It should go without saying that the three Ps should not be averaged into one report card grade"* (p. 135, emphasis in original).

Why is this important? We've all heard the expression of giving someone an "E for effort." Of course, this remark invariably accompanies a *failed* effort. Imagine what would happen if we combined performance and effort into a single metric. If we weighted the two equally and used the traditional A-to-F grading framework, we would arrive at a C. Reporting such a grade might be comforting in some ways because it takes into account the fact that the student was fully engaged and trying hard. But it would send the wrong signal both to parents and to the student. It's far more honest, and certainly more accurate, to report them separately. In this way, we can still acknowledge the effort a student has made without combining it with achievement (in an attempt to soften the bad news).

Figure 5.2 shows how separate marking systems might be used to indicate the differences (Jung & Guskey, 2012, p. 25). Note that different grading systems are used for product and process grades. This practice encourages a parent not to make direct comparisons between the two but to consider them separately.

Moving Toward Standards-Based Grading

We applaud the idea of reporting both product and process grades—and keeping them separate. However, we see the example in Figure 5.2 as only one step in the direction of true standards-based grading. The remaining steps involve reporting a student's status in terms of the standards themselves. For example, Shanahan (2015) recommends that at least two grades be assigned, one for foundational skills and another for reading defined more broadly (to include comprehension, learning from texts, understanding genres, and so forth). He points out that breaking down the subject of reading in this manner is consistent with the CCSS, where the same division occurs.

Of course, these domains can be broken down still further into standards. Shanahan (2015) warns against going overboard in this direction, however. There is a risk that including a large number of grades might overwhelm parents. In addition, teachers would be hard pressed to find evidence for some of them. When mandated to assign grades on the basis of sketchy and incomplete evidence, teachers will inevitably do their best, but accuracy may suffer. "If the information won't be accurate—and there is no way that teachers can adequately evaluate all of those individual standards—and won't be useful for aiming teachers and parents at addressing student needs, then there is no reason to have it on the report card" (Shanahan, 2015, paragraph 7).

We argue, however, that the key ELA Standards are not so numerous that they involve the risk of confusing parents. Our colleagues in Jefferson County, Georgia, have developed a report card that makes this point quite well. The kindergarten form appears in Figure 5.3. As you can see, the grades are clearly categorized and easy to follow.

Student:		Standard Marks		Process Marks	
Reporting Period:		4	Exemplary	++	Consistently
	1st	3	Proficient	+	Sometimes
	2nd	2	Progressing	−	Rarely
	3rd	1	Struggling	N/A	Not Assessed
	4th	N/A	Not Assessed		
		Modified standard. See progress report.			
Teacher:		**Language Arts**			
[Student's photo]		**Standard Goals**		**Process Goals**	
		Reading		*Preparation*	
		Writing		*Participation*	
		Listening		*Homework*	
		Speaking		*Cooperation*	
		Language		*Respect*	
Description and Comments:					

FIGURE 5.2. A report card that distinguishes product from process. From Jung and Guskey (2012). Copyright 2012 by Corwin Press. All rights reserved.

Reporting Periods	1	2	3	4
Language Arts				
Foundational Reading Skills				
Demonstrates concepts of print (left to right, top to bottom, letters vs. words, spacing between words, etc.)				
Names all upper- and lower-case letters				
Recognizes and produces rhyming words				
Blends and segments one-syllable words	▓			
Isolates and pronounces beginning, middle, end sounds in three-letter words	▓			
Knows consonant sounds				
Knows short-vowel sounds				
Reads common high-frequency words				
Reading—*Students must read both literary text and informational texts. All of these standards are with adult support.*				
Asks and answers questions about key details				
Identifies characters, setting, and major events				
Identifies the author and the illustrator and the roles they play				
Writing—*Uses a combination of drawing, dictating, and writing*				
Writes opinion pieces giving topic and an opinion	▓			
Writes informative texts giving the topic and some information about the topic	▓			
Writes narratives about a single event or closely linked events	▓			
With guidance and support adds details to strengthen writing	▓	▓		
With guidance and support explores digital tools to publish writing	▓	▓		
Participates in shared research and writing projects	▓	▓		
Language—*Demonstrates command of standard English grammar and conventions*				
Prints upper- and lower-case letters	▓			
Forms plurals appropriately	▓	▓		
Capitalizes first word in a sentence	▓			
Capitalizes word *I*	▓			
Recognizes and names end punctuation	▓			
Spells simple words phonetically	▓			

Scoring Guide:
- 4 = Exceeds the Standard
- 3 = Meets the Standard
- 2 = Progressing
- 1 = Emerging

FIGURE 5.3. Sample standards-based report card for kindergarten ELA. From M. Howard (personal communication, 2016).

Moving from Data to Grades

In our experience, many teachers prefer assigning report card grades on the basis of their overall impressions of a student's performance across the marking period. We do not doubt some teachers arrive at accurate judgments on this basis, but it is not a practice we recommend. As Conley (2005) notes, "Elementary schools appear to go out of their way to create grading systems that are not quantified" (p. 146). The result, he contends, is often a disconnect between grading and standards. Guskey and Jung (2013) point out that such a disconnect can extend to testing as well. Including nonacademic factors in a grade, they argue, accounts in part for the not uncommon discrepancy between a child's grades and performance on high-stakes assessments.

Consider an example from the report card shown in Figure 5.3. A kindergarten teacher must evaluate a student's ability to "name all upper- and lower-case letters." The teacher has undoubtedly observed the student during various alphabet activities and may have arrived at the general impression that every letter can be recognized. But administering a simple alphabet inventory would remove the guesswork and enable the teacher to award a 3.

But wait. Would you have awarded a 4? Note that in this case the standard simply requires that all letters be named. It is not possible to exceed the standard, which is what a grade of 4 would indicate. It is important that all kindergarten teachers faced with assigning this grade reach the same conclusion. For this reason, teachers need a grading guide to assist them in completing the report card. For every standard to be graded, teachers need consistent guidelines if they are to arrive at similar conclusions.

The example of letter naming is easy to quantify. The same cannot be said for many of the other standards, however. For instance, each child is expected to "identify characters, setting, and main events of a story." Evaluating the ability to do so is not nearly as straightforward as counting the number of letters a child can name. Agreeing on one story to be used near the end of the marking period by all teachers is a first step. The next is to decide on questions to ask and to develop a rubric for judging the responses.

In the case of writing, an agreed-upon writing prompt will produce the evidence needed to arrive at a grade. But the process of interpreting the written product must also be mutually understood by teachers. One of the kindergarten standards shown in Figure 5.3 requires that a student be able to "write informative texts giving the topic and some information about the topic." The question, of course, is how well a student can perform this task, for the standard at kindergarten will differ from the corresponding standard at second grade. Here, a combination of rubrics and end-of-year exemplar texts meeting the standard are necessary. The teacher's job is to compare each child's response to the prompt with the exemplar on a variety of characteristics, each associated with a rubric. Ideally, all teachers at the same grade level in a school will then be able to arrive at similar judgments of the same written product. A combination of exemplars and rubrics is the best option for evaluating a student's performance relative to a standard (Wiggins, 1994).

As we noted in Chapter 4, there is a key difference between standards for constrained and unconstrained proficiencies. In areas such as reading comprehension and writing, unlike letter naming, there is no such thing as achieving "mastery." This is because the bar rises as children move forward. More is expected of them in writing informative texts, for example, as they move from one grade to the next. This means we must use new and more challenging exemplars at each grade level. The same is true of many standards that are easier to quantify, such as oral reading fluency. As children move from the beginning to the middle to the end of a grade, the benchmarks change and with them the grades a teacher might assign.

To sum up, a grading guide makes it possible for all of the teachers on a grade-level team to reach similar conclusions as they assign grades that reflect student performance. Developing such a guide requires that decisions be made concerning what evidence to collect, when to collect it, and how to interpret it. The evidence can include numerical scores and rubrics; it should not include subjective impressions.

The time required to develop such a guide will be rewarded in a number of ways. Grading will be more objective and easier to explain to parents. The process is likely to provide valuable insights into each student's strengths and needs. And the use of a common approach will assist teachers in communicating with one another, which in turn will contribute to a shared sense of the role of grades and grading in a school. In a very real sense, it will help establish a school's "brand" for grading. In Figure 5.4, we outline the process.

Grading Student Progress

Figure 5.2 provides an example of how product and process grades can be reported together, without combining them. But what about the third "P"—progress? Assigning progress grades can sometimes provide a helpful context for a student who has failed to meet a particular standard. As an example, consider the case of oral reading fluency at second grade. Figure 5.5 gives the results for the DIBELS Next Oral Reading Fluency subtest (DORF) for two students, Robin and Pat, in the same class at the beginning and midyear benchmarking points. The beginning benchmark is 52 words correctly read per minute (WCPM), and the midyear benchmark is 72. Neither of these students met the benchmark at either time, and their teacher must indicate this fact in reporting on this standard. Robin, however, has made considerably more progress than Pat and is in fact nearing the standard.

Communicating not only performance at the end of the marking period but progress during that time is information that can be helpful to parents, and it is certainly instrumental in an RTI framework. The downside is the time and

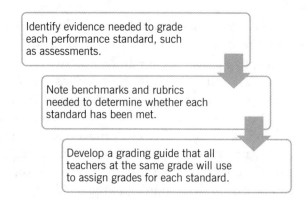

FIGURE 5.4. Guidelines for translating data into grades.

measurement problems required to estimate progress. Some standards lend themselves more easily than others to progress reporting, and they are likewise more central to RTI decisions. Whether progress grades should be formally built into report cards or reported separately and selectively is debatable.

Report Cards for Exceptional and Struggling Students

For students with individualized education plans (IEPs) or students who are English learners, Jung and Guskey (2012) recommend that grading follow a specific logic model. To begin with, a teacher should ask whether a standard is appropriate without any adaptation. If this is the case, the grading system used with other students is appropriate.

However, if an adaptation is required, a teacher should make a distinction between an accommodation and a modification. An accommodation is an adaptation that allows the student to acquire the same proficiencies as other students but in a manner that overcomes some difficulty. In the case of a visually impaired student, for example, an accommodation might involve the use of enlarged print. Accommodations do not necessitate any change in the grading system used for other students.

Student	Fall WCPM (52)	Winter WCPM (72)	Gain
Pat	33	43	10
Robin	38	65	27

FIGURE 5.5. Example of how a progress grade might be helpful.

A modification, on the other hand, is an adaptation that alters the standard in some fundamental way. For example, a student who has been resistant to intensive decoding interventions may benefit from a modification that entails having texts read aloud by a teacher or by text-to-speech software. Likewise, a student with limited English proficiency might benefit from adapted texts that include first-language equivalents of key words, available in the margins or on a touch-screen basis. In cases like these, the expectation for the student is not the same as for other students. Grades must be determined on the basis of the modified expectation, and their meaning must be clearly communicated to parents and other teachers. As Muñoz and Guskey (2015) note, "Report cards . . . should allow teachers to attach custom-scoring criteria for students who may be working on modified and/ or accommodated standards" (p. 67).

Summary

We recognize that moving to a standards-based report card might cause a bit of trepidation for teachers and administrators worried about how parents might react. When the transition is clearly communicated, however, such fears are mostly groundless. Swan, Guskey, and Jung (2014) compared parents' reactions to traditional versus standards-based report cards and found that parents overwhelmingly preferred the latter. Teachers and school leaders must think through the transition, of course, and provide opportunities to explain the new system and justify its use. That said, transitioning can be relatively smooth as long as certain guidelines are observed. We summarize these in Figure 5.6.

---

1. Avoid awarding a single grade in reading.

2. Grade the product (achievement or performance) separately from process and progress factors.

3. Award a product grade for each reading standard.

4. Develop a grading guide—a clear plan for using data to arrive at a product grade for each standard.

5. Offer straightforward guidance to parents about how to interpret the report card.

6. Include an invitation to confer.

7. Provide a space for parent comments.

8. Develop a clear grading policy for students receiving modifications.

FIGURE 5.6. Guidelines for developing a standards-based report card.

CHAPTER 6

· · · · · · · · · · ·

Organizing Your Space

GUIDING QUESTIONS
· ·

- Why is it important to consider space in primary classrooms?
- Which aspects of space are important to consider?
- How can you evaluate your classroom environment?
- What steps can you take to improve it?

Our visits to literally hundreds of preschool and primary classrooms have convinced us that teachers have a great many ideas about how to set up a classroom. From the arrangement of furniture to the storage of materials to the displays on walls, the variety is endless. Are these variations merely a matter of personal expression that don't affect achievement in any meaningful way? We believe that primary teachers should be free to create a physical environment that they believe to be warm, inviting, and conducive to learning. Up to a point, that is. As long as a number of guidelines are followed, there is plenty of opportunity for creative expression. In this chapter, we examine these guidelines. Some we regard as non-negotiable. Others are derived from research. Still others are practical recommendations that simply make good sense in light of learning objectives. We are not suggesting that anything like the mystic power of *feng shui* is required! We do claim that thinking about your own classroom as you read can be helpful.

Understanding Why Space Is Important
· ·

Let's begin by defining our target, the classroom environment. Some have defined it broadly to include not simply books, materials, and physical organization, but instruction, language use, curriculum and other elements. For example, the Early Language and Literacy Classroom Observation (ELLCO; Smith, Dickinson, Sangeorge, & Anastasopoulos, 2002) is a comprehensive evaluation tool that targets all of these elements. In this chapter, we have taken a narrower approach because the topics assessed by ELLCO are discussed in detail by the contributing authors to The Essential Library of PreK–2 Literacy. In other words, we will narrow the scope of the environment to what we can observe when the children and the teacher are not in the room.

A second reason for this approach is one that is all too frequently ignored. Lesley Morrow (2014) warns of the unfortunate tendency to overlook the classroom environment and focus instead on instructional strategies. This is a mistake, she argues. Teachers should arrange space and materials in a way that facilitates learning while creating a visual atmosphere that promotes literacy.

Here are a few assumptions about how the primary classroom environment can contribute to children's learning:

- Exposing children to large amounts of high-quality literature is essential.
- Each classroom must also facilitate whole-class and small-group instruction plus independent practice.
- The classroom design must allow smooth transitions between activities.
- Research on the best way to arrange a classroom environment can be useful to coaches and teachers.
- Existing research provides some clear lessons.

Safety First

The first priority of all teachers is to keep their children safe. By taking a few simple (and non-negotiable) precautions, you can ensure that the physical environment of your classroom helps you achieve this goal.

Think first about your field of vision. Make sure you can see all of the children all of the time. Avoid using furniture to create blind spots that prevent you from monitoring even a single child. Secluded nooks may have the appeal of privacy, but they are not worth the risk. Likewise, if you use a kidney-shaped table for small-group work, position it so that your back is near a wall or corner so that you can look over the heads of the children seated before you and keep an eye on all the others.

Think also about the materials stored about your room. Remember that some may present a temptation to curious children. Avoid stacking heavy materials on top of shelves—especially materials that children might want to access or use. Place the heaviest materials nearest the floor. Figure 6.1 displays a few of the problems that we frequently see but that are easily avoided. The shapes in the figure are usually bookcases.

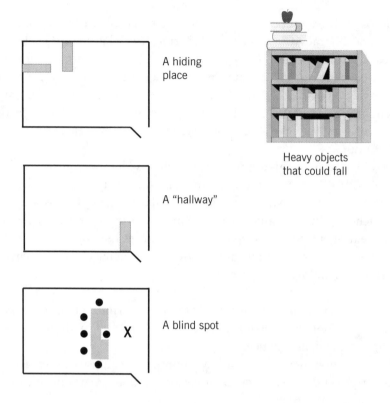

FIGURE 6.1. Safety concerns in the classroom environment.

Research on Effective Classroom Arrangement

Researchers have examined the connection between the physical environment of a classroom and student achievement. Their findings confirm not only that the two are linked (e.g., Neuman & Roskos, 1992) but that the results are consistent across the primary grades. For example, immersion in a print-rich environment has been found to be conducive to literacy growth (e.g., Reutzel & Wolfersberger, 1996), and children read more when more print is available inside the classroom (Morrow, 1990).

On a broad level, Reutzel and Wolfersberger (1996) have offered four principles of classroom design based on their summary of research. Findings have revealed that children's literacy learning is affected by:

1. The presence or absence of literacy tools.
2. The arrangement of space and the placement of literacy tools within the arranged space.
3. Social interaction among children as they use the literacy tools.
4. The authenticity of the context into which the literacy tools are placed.

From Research to Practice
. . . .

Reutzel and Wolfersberger offer a number of recommendations based on these principles:

- Stock your classroom with plenty of print, *but*
- Position most literacy materials in one area,
- Include a variety of writing utensils and surfaces,
- Change literacy tools and displays frequently,
- Create a library corner (literacy center).

Let's examine the idea of literacy and other centers a bit more closely. Lesley Morrow (2002) has devoted an entire book to the subject, and we've attempted to distill some of the most important recommendations here:

- Remember that the size of the center varies with the classroom and that in smaller classrooms the center may simply house materials, which are taken elsewhere to be used.
- Position "quiet" centers away from "active" ones.
- Use furniture to create a sense of privacy and physical definition.
- Consider including a "private spot" (but one that is always visible to you).
- Display children's writing prominently.
- Display posters that promote reading.
- Try to create a homelike environment (include pillows, rugs, rockers, bean-bag chairs, stuffed animals, etc.).
- Include both fiction and nonfiction books, labeled by type, topic, and/or level.
- Introduce the class to new additions to the center throughout the year. Don't simply add them without comment.
- Include manipulatives (puppets, props, felt board, headsets and CD players, word study materials).
- Include functional print, such as
   o Labels ("Books about Science") and
   o Directions ("Quiet please," "Please put materials away after using them").
- Include environmental print (e.g., word walls) and give children chances to use it.

Classrooms should be set up so that children know how to find what they need easily and quickly. "All materials that children need are accessible," Morrow observes about a productive preschool classroom environment. "Furthermore, all materials have their own special spots. Various containers with labels are used to organize materials the children use" (2007, p. 4). We believe it's fair to extend the same idea to classrooms throughout the primary grades. Organization saves time and helps to minimize distractions. It also creates community because all children are empowered to use and to put away materials.

McGee and Richgels (2014) have compiled a number of additional recommendations concerning the physical environment of the primary classroom. We summarize a few of their most important points:

- When small spaces suggest a specific theme (such as a library corner), children are more likely to behave accordingly.
- When spaces are linked to specific activities, it is easier to teach routines, such as transitions.
- Tables tend to work better than desks (assuming you have a choice) because they facilitate different kinds of activities, from eating snacks to art projects to partner reading.
- An institutional look can be overcome through the use of soft lamps, pillows, rugs, and plants.
- Bringing in materials from the outside can make the space even more distinctive and pique curiosity at the same time.

Components of a Productive Literacy Environment

An important first step in sizing up a primary classroom environment is through the use of a checklist. Such a tool can help you appraise the general quality of the children's literacy surroundings and, more importantly, identify gaps and weaknesses. Hoffman, Sailors, Duffy, and Beretvas (2004) offer a useful checklist as part of their TEX-IN3 instrument (named perhaps as a pun because of the authors' ties to the University of Texas). Figure 6.2 lists the 17 categories of texts they consider most important. Think about the prevalence of each in your own classroom and about the message your text resources communicates to your class about reading and writing.

Judging the Local Text Environment

As you examined the categories, you may have been surprised at the inclusion of so many items other than books. To be sure, books are the most important component of a print-rich early literacy classroom, but they aren't the only one. Also important are texts produced "locally"—by you and your students. These must be given a prominent place in the classroom environment. Hoffman and his colleagues (2004) suggest that "local" texts include any material written by students, the teacher, or a combination of both. For example, a writing prompt written by

1. **Computers/electronic texts.** This category includes any texts that are accessed and used through an electronic medium. *Examples:* Messaging systems (e-mail), Internet access (for research), software programs (reading and authoring programs), tests or test preparation, text files that are saved and accessed by students, books-on-tape (e.g., listening centers), and news or information shows.

2. **Extended text process charts.** These are multisentence, connected texts that are procedural and guide students toward the use of a particular process or strategy. Some of them may be ongoing. *Examples:* Language charts, inquiry charts, writing process charts, math strategies or algorithms, rubrics.

3. **Games/puzzles/manipulatives.** These are instructional materials designed for student use (often as independent or small-group work). To be considered in this category they must feature text prominently. *Examples:* Bingo, *Clue*, word sorts, magnetic poetry.

4. **Instructional aids.** Often these charts are used as a visual aid to support direct instruction or mini-lessons. They may remain displayed in the classroom after a lesson and be used as an artifact for that lesson or as a reference point for students (e.g., a color chart). Instructional Aid Charts focus on content while Process Charts focus on process. *Examples:* Poems for reading together, morning message, labels, vocabulary lists.

5. **Journals.** Journals must be "local" texts created by the students (individuals or groups working together) based primarily on their work and writing. *Examples:* Personal journals, literature response logs, content inquiry logs (math, science, and social studies), draft writing.

6. **Leveled books.** These texts are created explicitly for instruction in reading and are leveled for difficulty and accessibility. Basal readers tend to be collections of short selections bound together and include carefully controlled vocabulary (either literature-based anthologies or skills-driven selections). "Little books" tend to be bound single selections that are carefully leveled (and even numbered) in terms of accessibility. *Examples:* "Little books," decodable books.

7. **Limited text process charts.** This category includes letter/word level texts that are procedural and guide the students in the use of a particular strategy or set of strategies. These are similar to the Extended Text Charts in purpose and design; however, they tend to focus at the letter or word level. *Examples:* Word walls, alphabet charts, spelling "demon" charts.

8. **Organizational/management charts.** These displays are used to manage or organize the social, academic, or curricular work within the classroom. *Examples:* Student-helpers chart, workboards, class rules, and local or state curricular objectives, a chart for multiplication facts mastered by students, a skill mastery chart, a record of number of books read.

9. **Portfolios.** Student portfolios are locations for and an organizer for the work completed by students. Consider when looking at portfolios the range of texts collected, the processes of collecting texts, the access and use of these texts, and issues of control over these texts (e.g., what gets in, how, when).

10. **Reference materials.** These are materials that are used as resources for finding information (e.g., word spellings, locations, how to do something). *Examples:* Atlas, dictionary, encyclopedia, English grammar handbook, thesaurus, globe, maps.

(continued)

FIGURE 6.2. TEX-IN3 text types. From Hoffman, Sailors, Duffy, and Beretvas (2004). Copyright 2004 by Sage Publications. All rights reserved.

---

11. **Serials.** This text type includes a variety of locally and imported materials. Consideration of these texts should focus on qualities of topical relevance, accessibility for the students, quality of the publication, and the number of copies available (Is there one for every student? Is it promoted as a reference or on display?). *Examples: Ranger Rick, Highlights,* Scholastic newspapers, classroom newspapers, school and community newsletters.

12. **Social/personal/motivational displays.** These might include motivational posters about reading, student of the week displays, current events bulletin boards, etc. *Examples:* Text innovations with big books, individual-student-authored books, reports/inquiry projects.

13. **Student/teacher published work.** This category consists of locally authored (by a student, a teacher, or a combination of the two) books or publications and are on display for students to use. These texts tend to be more permanent than Work Product Displays. *Examples:* Text innovations with big books, individual-student-authored books, reports/inquiry projects.

14. **Textbooks.** These are student texts that are typically identified with a subject/content area. Textbooks in this category have a clear instructional design for the teacher to use and the students to follow in learning new concepts and skills. Basal readers are not included in this category. *Examples:* Mathematics textbooks, science textbooks, English grammar books, basal readers.

15. **Tradebooks.** These books do not have an obvious instructional design; they are often called "library books" or "children's literature." *Examples:* Picture books and chapter books; narrative, expository, and procedural texts.

16. **Work product displays.** These are displays of teacher or student work that is being "celebrated" and set forward for others to read and enjoy. *Examples:* Model writing samples.

17. **Writing on paper.** These texts involve a written response on paper. These responses vary across a wide continuum, ranging from tightly constrained text response formats to entirely open-ended response/writing formats. Creative writing activities to literature responses to math problem solving exercises. Workbooks are also included in this category. *Examples:* Reading, math, phonics, and spelling workbooks/worksheets; blank paper with assigned topics to write from; paper for creative writing.

FIGURE 6.2. *(continued)*

the teacher on chart paper would be a local teacher text, as would a word wall or a vocabulary chart (see Figure 6.3). In fact, our favorite primary classrooms are so filled with these local texts that there is actually no room for any commercially produced ones.

Likewise, a response journal or a student-authored storybook would be examples of local student texts. Hoffman and his colleagues make a further distinction between local student texts and mere work product displays (see Figure 6.2). The latter typically include daily assignments and are quite limited in nature. Figure 6.4 provides the 5-point rubric the authors suggest for judging the local texts in evidence. You will see that their rubric is consistent with our biases about the importance and richness of these teacher-made texts. Take a look around your room and use the rubric to conduct a self-appraisal.

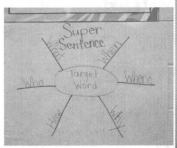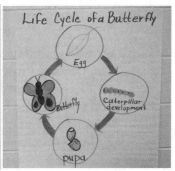

FIGURE 6.3. Examples of local texts.

---

5. Extremely rich. Local Texts are visible everywhere in the classroom and are a pervasive part of the classroom literacy environment. There is a nice balance between teacher-authored and student-authored texts. The teacher and the students appear to use these texts actively in support of their learning. The local texts are in evidence across many areas of the curriculum, are used procedurally (e.g., in management and classroom routines) and support of content learning. There are local texts in various stages of development in the classroom. The local texts may not all have a "published" look about them. Rather, they are designed with student use in mind. Both public and private local texts are used in the classroom. Students have opportunities to author these texts in open-ended ways rather than just "complete" them.

4. Rich. The number and variety of local texts is more limited, but evidence is clear that the local texts are created, valued, and used regularly by the students and the teacher. Both extended and limited local texts are in use. The students also use public and private texts actively. The local texts are more open-ended than closed in the response opportunities. Students clearly engage actively and regularly with these texts.

3. Functional. Some local texts are featured in the classroom. The public local texts tend to be fairly closed in terms of student input and ownership. They tend to be mainly tied to the reading/language arts curriculum or fairly routine/procedural activities (e.g., calendar, weather, book check-out systems).

2. Limited. The local texts are limited in number and tend toward the functional and the display variety. There is little evidence of their dynamic use. Private local texts are structured or used infrequently. They show little evidence of creative input of the children. There may be almost a careless or haphazard look in their design features.

1. Inadequate. There are no local texts featured in prominent ways. There may be some routine charts and graphs, but these are largely functional in nature and teacher controlled.

FIGURE 6.4. TEX-IN3 rubric for the local text environment. From Hoffman, Sailors, Duffy, and Beretvas (2004). Copyright 2004 by Sage Publications. All rights reserved.

Judging Other Print-Related Materials

A still broader definition of print-related materials can be assessed through the Classroom Literacy Environmental Profile (CLEP; Wolfersberger, Reutzel, Sudweeks, & Fawson, 2004). In addition to books, the CLEP permits a systematic examination of writing implements, cards, chart paper, and many other items useful in promoting literacy. The CLEP is too extensive to be reprinted here, but we encourage grade-level teams to consider it as they take stock together of their classroom environments. Fortunately, instruments like the CLEP and the TEX-IN3 rubrics can be applied even when school is not in session.

Deciding Where Activities Should Take Place

The primary classroom should accommodate a combination of whole-class, small-group, and individual literacy activities. From prekindergarten through grade 2, we encourage you to conduct whole-class activities away from tables, desks, and chairs unless students are sharing books or writing. Establishing an open space containing a rug, a comfortable chair, a marker board, and an easel will enable you to conduct activities using an up-close-and-personal approach. Teacher read-alouds are more engaging and can be made more interactive. For example, partners can be asked to share thoughts and make predictions at strategic points ("Turn to your partner and . . ."). Because it is essential for children to see illustrations in books that a teacher reads aloud (especially picture books or nearly any type of nonfiction), sitting at close range is important. The same is true for dialogic shared reading, which typically involves big (or projected) books in preschool and kindergarten. In shared reading, students must be able to see not only the graphics but the text.

From a common area used for whole-class instruction, students must be able to transition quickly and efficiently to locations designated for individual and small-group work. The literacy center is one such location. Others include tables or desks and a kidney-shaped table like the one shown in Figure 6.5 reserved for small-group work. (Notice, too, how the teacher has positioned it to prevent a blind spot.) Early in the year, teachers must provide explicit instruction in how to move from one activity to another, and the room setup must facilitate orderly movement. Moreover, the room arrangement should remain the same throughout the year. There are many ways to introduce novelty and variety into your instruction without upsetting the apple cart from time to time, making it necessary for students to relearn transitions. Routines are important, and a constant room arrangement helps establish them.

The literacy center itself can be used in several ways. During designated times, it can serve as a miniature lending library where students can select books. It can

FIGURE 6.5. Rachel Simpkins has positioned her small-group table so that she can keep an eye on all of her kindergartners. Photo by Ginger Parris.

also be a place for independent reading, where some students may feel especially comfortable. For students who are reading the same book, the literacy center can also be an excellent place to discuss it in a small group (or literature circle) as you work with other groups.

Summary

In just a few pages, we've offered a great many suggestions for effectively arranging your classroom, from positioning furniture to storing books. We also suggested resources to help you judge the quantity and quality of literacy materials. The TEX-IN3 rubrics can assist you in evaluating both the local and classroom environment of books. The CLEP can take you a step further, gauging the availability of many literacy-related materials. We asked that you contrast these suggestions as you read with your own physical classroom. In doing so, you can identify areas where improvements can make a major difference in the impact you make as a teacher.

CHAPTER 7

Organizing Your Time

- How can you balance time for whole-class and differentiated instruction?
- How can you balance time for reading and for writing?
- How can you use ELA time to build social studies and science knowledge?

We hear it everywhere we go. There just isn't enough time for everything. That's definitely true. Time is surely a limited resource, and it's one that we have to budget very carefully. As with any budgeting exercise, we start with broad categories (utilities, auto expenses), and then we get very specific (water, electricity, garbage or car payment, insurance, gas). In this chapter, we will do both. We will also discuss the elephant in the room: differentiation. We will argue that, contrary to some teacher evaluation systems, it is actually impossible to differentiate every part of every lesson. In fact, we think that undifferentiated grade-level instruction should be at the heart of your literacy block, augmented with carefully-thought-out differentiation.

Making Time for Teaching and Learning
. . . .

How much time do you actually have? According to the National Center for Education Statistics' (NCES; 2005) School and Staffing Survey, the average number of minutes in a school day is 398, just over 6½ hours. In case you're interested, the average elementary class size is 21.6 for a self-contained class and 26.2 for a departmentalized class. You can find all kinds of facts about the profession at the NCES website (*https://nces.ed.gov*). Most data are available by state and on average.

What does 6½ hours look like in a schedule? To us, it's eight 45-minute blocks of time with 30 minutes left over. Figure 7.1 apportions those blocks. In a school day, then, it is theoretically possible to have three segments (135 minutes) for literacy, two (90 minutes) for math, 45 minutes for either science or social studies, and 45 minutes for a daily special. Although we agree that both science and social studies are important knowledge builders, we also think that you can integrate important content from both areas into your reading and your read-alouds. We realize that there are no built-in bathroom or fountain breaks, but once rituals and routines are established, it is much more efficient to have those happen as needed instead of devoting large segments of instructional time to having children wait their turns in bathroom lines.

You will see in the next chapter that we use these set blocks of 45 minutes for several reasons. First, if the "parts" of the school day are the same size, it's easier to make a staggered schedule to make good use of specialists. We will take on that challenge in Chapter 8. The order of these segments doesn't matter. Some members of your team can teach math first. Others can have differentiation before reading. Lunch and recess are together so that one group can be ruling the playground while another is going through the lunch line. Realistically, nearly all schools already have a 90-minute literacy block and a 30- to 45-minute intervention block, so the extra 15 minutes is not unrealistic.

15 minutes	• Morning Routine
45 minutes	• Shared Reading
45 minutes	• Read-Aloud and Writing
45 minutes	• Differentiation and Intervention
45 minutes	• Lunch and Recess
45 minutes	• Math
45 minutes	• Math
45 minutes	• Science or Social Studies
45 minutes	• Music, Art, Physical Education, Library, Computer Lab
15 minutes	• Pack Up

FIGURE 7.1. Possible schedule for school day.

Planning Your Shared Reading Block

We have been calling the reading block "shared reading." What we mean when we use that term is that it is whole-class, grade-level, standards-based instruction. It definitely centers on text, and that text is carefully selected. If you have used a commercial reading program, that text is the grade-level story. We think that existing commercial core programs have too little text to produce the accelerated achievement required by the new standards, so we favor the use of tradebooks instead. Or if you have to use a commercial core, you might be able to use it for the first half of the school year and then use tradebooks for the second half. Regardless of your materials, you have to have grade-level text to ground your shared reading.

Shared Reading in Preschool and Kindergarten

Our smallest learners are a special case here, but we include them because kindergartners are part of the school community, and many preschool classes are finding their way into elementary buildings. They certainly cannot spend 45 minutes in whole-class instruction! For them, we think of three 10- to 15-minute blocks with dancing or exercise in between. For preschool teachers, one big book and three or more centers are necessary for each week of the year. For kindergarten teachers, one big book per week, a visible alphabet, a set of poems and songs, and picture cards are the necessary supplies. Figure 7.2 provides an overview.

Another difference is the amount of repetition. Preschool and kindergarten children need more repetition. Think of the young children to whom you have read at home. They want the same books over and over again. This natural inclination no doubt fuels their language development and helps them enter the world of story.

We think that the essential routine for shared reading in preschool and kindergarten is dialogic reading. The good news is that dialogic reading has the strongest research base in the read-aloud literature (Swanson et al., 2011). Although its

	Preschool	Kindergarten
15 minutes	Dialogic reading	Dialogic reading
5 minutes	Wiggle Time	
10 minutes	Centers	Alphabet and Phonological Awareness
5 minutes	Wiggle Time	
10 minutes	Centers	Tracking Text

FIGURE 7.2. Shared reading in preschool and kindergarten.

emphasis is on oral language, dialogic reading also builds print concepts, phono-logical awareness, comprehension, and vocabulary, even for children at risk for reading difficulty. Still better news is that dialogic reading is among the most natural and enjoyable things that teachers and children can do together in school. That makes sense because it is founded on the essential interactions that occur as a caregiver reads to a young child sitting on his or her lap.

In a dialogic reading, children do most of the talking (Ezell & Justice, 2005; Lonigan & Whitehurst, 1998). It is not didactic; it is not predictable. It is a free-wheeling (and usually quite entertaining) discussion. The trick is to learn to ask children questions for which there are many possible answers and to use their answers as a way to expand their language. We have worked with teachers to make this type of reading the cornerstone of shared reading by helping them choose one book for each week of the year. The book can be a big book or a regular book projected so that all of the children can see it. It has to have great illustrations and a sequential structure. In order for it to be interesting for a whole week, it shouldn't be simple or repetitive enough for children to memorize. Figure 7.3 provides our weekly schedule for planning dialogic reading.

You will see in our organizer that things diverge after dialogic reading. Pre-schoolers move into centers. For us, centers are places where adults engage with children in language as the children play. The trick is getting the adults to engage. Most preschool classrooms have at least two adults present at all times. They should both be engaged in language development in different centers. With three centers (perhaps a puppet stage, a restaurant, and blocks, to start), one adult can talk with children in the restaurant and the other adult can interact with those who are building, leaving the puppet stage as a child-only center that day. After a wiggle and transition, the children can choose a different center, so that all would have at least one 10-minute block with an adult language partner, and many chil-dren would have two.

For kindergarten, that second chunk of shared reading is alphabet and pho-nological awareness. It includes both alphabet work and phonological awareness work in the context of a song or poem. We favor 4 weeks of natural, playful work with the entire alphabet (singing it, saying the letter names, and tracking it), fully modeled by the teacher. That routine, costing fewer than 5 minutes, gives all chil-dren a playful exposure to the entire alphabet before they isolate and master the names and shapes and sounds of each letter. After the first month of school, that full alphabet work should be replaced with 5 minutes of compare-and-contrast work, linking letter name instruction with the phonological skill of initial sound sorting.

Initial sound sorting should be a main emphasis in the first half of the kinder-garten year and linked directly with children's letter name and sound instruction. Regardless of tradition, there has never been any evidence that teaching one letter each week is effective. You have to teach them more quickly than that, and in sets.

Monday	Do a picture walk, asking *wh-* questions that allow the children to label the illustrations. • "Who do you think that is?" • "What do we call those?" • "Why is that happening?"
Tuesday	Read again, this time asking completion questions after each page or two. • "The boy was feeling _____." • "The author said that this was a _____." • "That character was wearing a _____."
Wednesday	Read again, this time asking recall questions after each page or two. • "What is going to happen next?" • "Why did the cat do that?" • "What is the big surprise?"
Thursday	Read again, this time asking open-ended or distancing questions after each page or two. • "What would you have done if you'd been there?" • "Have you ever seen anything like this?" • "How would you feel if that happened to you?"
Friday	Read again straight through. At the end of the reading, guide the children to construct a collaborative retelling. • "What happened in the beginning?" • "What happened in the middle?" • "What happened in the end?"

FIGURE 7.3. Dialogic reading. From *Organizing the Early Literacy Classroom: How to Plan for Success and Reach Your Goals* by Sharon Walpole and Michael C. McKenna. Copyright © 2016 The Guilford Press. Permission to photocopy this figure is granted to purchasers of this book for personal use or use with individual students. (see copyright page for details). Purchasers can download enlarged versions of this figure (see the box at the end of the table of contents).

Here's how it works: First you need a compare-and-contrast scope and sequence. Generally, you teach the most common sounds first, you avoid pairing letters that look similar (b, d, p, g, q), and you integrate the short vowels. In *Words Their Way: Word Study for Phonics, Vocabulary, and Spelling Instruction*, Bear, Invernizzi, Templeton, and Johnson (2015) provide useful direction. You teach the letter names and their sounds in initial position in words by picture sorting, modeling for children that you can listen to an orally presented word, isolate its first sound, and categorize that sound with other words that start the same. This routine combines initial phonics instruction (teaching letter names and sounds) with initial phonological awareness instruction (isolating and matching initial sounds).

We favor going much deeper than that with phonological awareness each day. Phonological awareness is an umbrella term for the ability to notice and manipulate the individual speech sounds in orally presented words. Children typically acquire phonological awareness sequentially, moving from noticing words, to

Monday	Tuesday	Wednesday	Thursday	Friday
Memorize poem or song	Count words and syllables	Find or produce rhyming words	Segment and blend onsets and rimes	Segment and blend phonemes

FIGURE 7.4. Using a song or poem to build phonological awareness through the week.

syllables within words, to onsets and rimes, to individual speech sounds (see, e.g., Lane, Pullen, & Eisele, 2002, for a description). However, given the achievement diversity in a typical kindergarten classroom, we prefer a playful approach at all of these levels during shared reading time. In the context of a song or poem, you can easily engage children in a rich language exploration, memorizing the text first and then isolating one particular phonological feature each day. Figure 7.4 provides a simple organizer.

The final chunk of shared reading time is tracking text: knowing how books work, that they have front and back covers, that we read the left page before the right, that text on each page runs from left to right and top to bottom, that words are separated from one another by spaces. These skills have to be automatic before we can actually teach children to attend to the parts of words (letters and sounds) that they will use to read conventionally. We favor a third text here, just to increase the volume of language and the variety in shared reading. A poem or nursery rhyme that children can memorize is perfect here, as long as it combines single-syllable and multisyllabic words. Figure 7.5 provides a possible plan.

Shared Reading in First and Second Grades

Shared reading in first and second grade has fewer moving parts than in the preschool and kindergarten years, mostly because we can engage these children in more conventional reading. And we mean to do that at very high volume. Shared reading is a time for supported, high-volume, contextualized practice. As in the

Monday	Tuesday	Wednesday	Thursday	Friday
Memorize poem or song	Model with a think-aloud where to start reading, how to match each spoken word to a printed one, and how to move from line to line.	Model with a think-aloud where to start reading, how to match each spoken word to a printed one, and how to move from line to line.	Engage children in tracking particular lines or stanzas.	Engage children in tracking particular lines or stanzas.

FIGURE 7.5. Phonological awareness play in context.

first two years of school, this practice centers on actual text, but the difference is in the repetitiveness. In preschool and kindergarten, we are repeating access to a weekly diet of big books, poems, and stories across the week, with slightly different purposes so that the children can make the move from emergent or pretend reading into conventional reading. Once they are reading conventionally (not by memorizing or guessing, but by processing the letters within words), it's all about practice.

Never before the CCSS overturned our organizational apple cart has text complexity been a hotter item. The CCSS mandate that children read "harder" text earlier in their careers. But what exactly makes a text easy or hard at the beginning reader stage? Decodable words? High-frequency words? Rhyming words? Words with concrete or familiar meanings? Simple sentence structures? Repetitive sentence structures? Repetitive clauses? Recent empirical research reveals that all of these things matter (Fitzgerald et al., 2015). When we choose books for first-grade shared reading, we choose what Kathleen Brown (1999) has called transitional readers and easy readers. These books are narratives with a combination of high-frequency, decodable, and familiar words. They are neither entirely predictable nor entirely decodable, but instead reinforce all of the skills that first-grade readers are acquiring.

I Can Read books are a good multiple-criterion series to consider for early first grade. They are organized by levels, include many, many titles, and feature some well-loved and memorable characters: Pete the Cat, Biscuit, Danny and the Dinosaur, Little Bear, Flat Stanley, Little Critter, and Frog and Toad are on our "must-read list" for first-grade shared reading. Because these books are published in series, you can also organize shared reading to include mini-author studies or to prompt a run on the media center.

First-grade shared reading can move into more complex chapter books at the end of the year. We have had success with early chapter book mysteries: Young Cam Jansen and Nate the Great. These books approach the Lexile scores identified in the CCSS Appendices to match the final anchor standards in literary and informational texts: reading grade-level text of sufficient complexity.

Beginning in second grade, we take Lexile scores as an important component in text selection for shared reading. A Lexile score is a quantitative measure of text difficulty that considers word frequency and sentence length. Lexiles are widely available. Visit Lexile.com to find scores for titles of interest. When we are choosing texts for second-grade shared reading, we look for titles with Lexiles between 400 and 600 in narratives with chapters and engaging characters and in information books that build social studies and science background knowledge.

Text selection is the most difficult aspect of shared reading in first and second grade. After that, it's about support and repetition. Figure 7.6 provides an organizational template. Think of the times that we assign to each task as proportions.

5 minutes	• Teach spelling and meaning vocabulary.
12 minutes	• Set a first purpose for reading and engage in echo or choral reading.
12 minutes	• Set a new purpose for reading and engage children in partner rereading.
10 minutes	• Hold a comprehension discussion.
6 minutes	• Create a class story map or summary. • Assign a text-based response.

FIGURE 7.6. Shared reading in first and second grades.

More than half of a 45-minute shared reading period has to be reserved for actual student reading. Our readers are novices, though, so that reading is supported in two ways. First, we rely on the fluency techniques that provide optimal teacher support: echo or choral reading. You are leading the children through the text, supporting their word recognition and their prosody. The second support is the immediate rereading. Even before the comprehension discussion, we have students paired to practice. After teaching routines for partner reading, including how to listen and provide help, you can engage your partners in practice while you circulate to monitor or provide another round of choral reading to accomplish that key repetition for students who need additional support. There is no doubt about it—repeated readings build fluency and comprehension (Samuels, 1979).

You may be wondering about comprehension instruction. We do not center our shared reading on a comprehension skill or strategy—or even on a particular standard. We center it on a text and that particular text's affordances. We recommend a dash of comprehension instruction in the form of modeling during shared reading, and then support of inferential thinking during the comprehension discussion after reading and in the design of a text-based response. We see shared reading segments dominated by comprehension strategy instruction *at the virtual exclusion of any student reading.* In a limited-resource system, we think time spent reading is more valuable than time spent listening to teachers talk about reading (Willingham & Lovette, 2014).

Our organizational plan for first- and second-grade shared reading is surprisingly simple. Teach spelling every day. Read new text every day with high levels of teacher support. Reread immediately with less support. Talk about the text at a deep level, informed by the two readings. Assess and deepen text comprehension through a text-based response that students complete after reading.

If you are thinking that shared reading does not sound very difficult or very different from what you have seen or done, you are probably right. The first real difference is in overall volume of text read and in the difficulty level at the end of the first-grade year. That is no small difference; many classrooms are simply not equipped with new materials to address new standards. New materials cost money, but adding trade books (instead of commercial core programs) is a much cheaper adjustment. As an added bonus, we have been ordering only enough copies for half the class to foster the partner relationships that support rereading. The second real difference is the end of worksheets and workbooks. You need waste no more money on these items. If this seems easy, then wait until we describe the next block!

Planning Your Read-Aloud and Writing Block

Teachers in the primary grades have always read aloud. As with shared reading, our organizational plan for a read-aloud and writing block makes subtle but substantive and powerful adjustments to that practice. The first one is this: We want you to pick more difficult books. For us, read-alouds are the main course in language and knowledge building as children are developing the skills they need to learn new things by reading on their own.

In our experience, primary grade teachers tend to choose books with strong rhyme, repetitive language, and familiar plot lines. Those books are fun to share with young children and they certainly foster phonological awareness. But how many of them deepen vocabulary and background knowledge and knowledge of the world? How many build science understanding? How many introduce historical times and figures? We argue that those language-play books are better used as part of kindergarten shared reading than as interactive read-alouds.

Interactive read-alouds are different from language play because the goal is to use a beautiful book to teach children things more complex than what they know and to expose them to more rare words and more varied syntax. What children listen to and talk about in the first years of schooling enables their reading and writing later. Although we have not been able to balance fiction and nonfiction shared reading, especially in first grade, we can balance it with interactives. Perhaps best yet, since you only need one copy, and you can get it from your school's or town's media center, there is virtually no cost involved.

Our plan for these read-alouds is simple and repetitive, but the devil is in the details. We have slightly different frames for narratives and information books. Figure 7.7 compares and contrasts the two approaches. The main differences revealed above are about vocabulary instruction and text structure instruction. For vocabulary, we follow the lead of Isabel Beck and her colleagues (e.g., Beck, McKeown, & Kucan, 2008). We teach Tier Two words—those words that provide nuanced labels for familiar concepts—*after* reading narratives. We teach Tier Three words—content-area specific words without which comprehension is

	Fiction	Nonfiction
Before Reading	• Ask partners to share written responses to yesterday's prompt.	• Ask partners to share written responses to yesterday's prompt.
	• Develop or activate background knowledge.	• Develop or activate background knowledge.
		• Preview technical vocabulary.
		• Introduce the text structure.
During Reading	• Ask questions during reading and model comprehension strategies.	• Ask questions during reading and model comprehension strategies.
After Reading	• Lead a brief discussion.	• Lead a brief discussion.
	• Teach Tier Two words.	
	• Lead the class in sentence composing.	• Lead the class in sentence composing.
	• Assign a written response after each day.	• Assign a written response after each day.

FIGURE 7.7. Planning frames for fiction and nonfiction interactive read-alouds.

impossible—before reading nonfiction. We also address text structures (description, sequence, comparison, topic-subtopic, problem and solution, or cause and effect) *before* reading to help young listeners identify and remember important text information and to acquaint them with how authors organize information.

You will see that we include sentence-composing activities at the end of each read-aloud. Sentence composing is a type of grammar instruction very different from your grandmother's. It is exciting, interactive, and creative, and it includes no diagrams or worksheets. If you are intrigued, first visit the webpage of Don and Jenny Killgallon (*http://userpages.umbc.edu/~killgall*) and then return to Chapter 2 and consider the titles that you might use to build your understanding here.

Assignment of a written response rounds out this portion of the block. We use these text-based responses both to deepen understanding and to assess it. As with our written responses for shared reading in grades 1 and 2, these responses should require inferential thinking. They should be open-ended and interesting to write and to read. They can combine drawing and words as children build their transcription skills. The difference is that these responses address listening comprehension instead of reading comprehension.

As you organize for instruction, we suggest that you apportion half of the school year for interactive read-aloud and grammar instruction and half for process writing in this particular block of time. As a field, our understanding of what it takes to teach writing is less sophisticated than our understanding of what it takes to teach reading. However, here are the take-home messages from a recent review (Graham et al., 2012):

1. Students need time to write each day. We are building in time for text-based writing after shared reading and interactive read-alouds, and we are also reserving 90 45-minute periods for full blocks of writing.

2. Students need to learn to use the writing process to produce different types of texts. Current standards balance persuasion, information, and narrative at all grade levels. These are the types of text to teach; the writing process is the recursive process of planning, drafting, revising, editing, and publishing.

3. Make sure that students are confident with the tools of writing: hand-writing, spelling, sentence construction, and eventually typing and word processing. We have been supporting the resurgence of formal handwriting instruction in the kindergarten block. We address spelling in shared reading. We target the sentence in our grammar instruction.

4. Connect your students to one another as a community of writers. We envision your writing periods as busy, noisy, collaborative work sessions with students working together to write.

Many of our university colleagues are publishing great new work on early writing. If this is an interest of yours, return to Chapter 2 to feed it.

Planning Your Differentiation Block

Two blocks down, one to go. The differentiation block is the one with which we have the longest history. It's easier to understand our approach now that you've read about the rest of the ELA time. We have structured 90 minutes of daily instructional time with virtually no direct instruction in skills. That's because we have learned that basic skills are more *quickly* developed in differentiated small groups. For a comprehensive look at our differentiation block, including nearly all of the materials you need to deliver it, see *How to Plan Differentiated Reading Instruction: Resources for Grades K–3* (Walpole & McKenna, 2009).

Here is the short story: Within a carefully organized block, centered on understanding rich, authentic texts, we can afford an entirely skills-based differentiation block. Figure 7.8 provides a visual representation. You may notice that it is slightly updated from the one in our differentiation book. That is because the standards have changed since then, and we have responded by designing shared and interactive read-aloud/writing blocks to balance our differentiation model. We hope you will agree that no students who have already mastered the decoding of single-syllable words get any more decoding instruction. Instead, they spend their time consolidating their skills in fluency work or expanding their background knowledge in yet another rich text.

Our differentiation model does not require assessments of instructional reading level or use of guided reading (Fountas & Pinnell, 1996). Instead of assigning children to leveled books, we have helped teachers to identify very specific skills-based targets for differentiation. You read in Chapter 4 that screenings and diagnostic assessments can work in tandem to identify instructional needs.

Our experience tells us that nearly all kindergartners who begin the basic alphabet knowledge lessons by the tenth week of school can master using letter patterns by the end of the kindergarten year. Many finish much more quickly, and we ask teachers to use differentiation time for them to listen to short texts read aloud, construct a common summary sentence, and practice their transcription skills by writing it.

First-grade students may very well start on the kindergarten step, but to develop the fluency required by the end of first grade and the beginning of second grade, they need to master vowel teams by the start of the fourth quarter of the first-grade year. Logically, then, second graders whose achievement data reveal they need instruction in kindergarten or first-grade skills are significantly at risk; they should be functioning at the fluency and comprehension or vocabulary and comprehension step by the start of the year (see Figure 7.8).

Always concerned with overall organization, we have designed our differentiation lessons to be 15 minutes long. That means that a single teacher can see three groups each day in a 45-minute differentiation block. While students are not meeting with the teacher, they can complete their written response to shared reading and interactive read-alouds or work on their process writing pieces. If they finish with their writing, they can read from the titles in the classroom library.

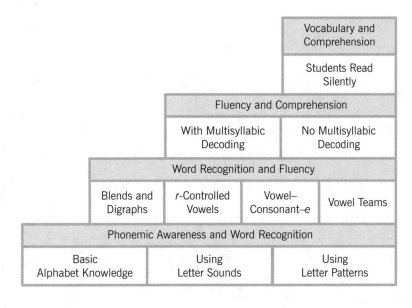

FIGURE 7.8. A staircase of skills-based differentiation.

Summary

We hope you are intrigued. We have designed a coherent ELA block that comprises three equal-time components: shared reading, interactive read-aloud/writing, and differentiation. Shared reading in preschool and kindergarten targets language development first and foremost, with a dash of foundational skills in kindergarten. In first and second grade, shared reading includes spelling instruction and supported fluency building. Interactive read-alouds for half the year build knowledge of all types, including grammar. And writing for half the year builds the capacity for children to use the writing process to compose narratives, information texts, and persuasive pieces.

CHAPTER 8
. . . .

Organizing Your Team

GUIDING QUESTIONS
. . . .

- What are the specialized roles of other adults who support teaching and learning?
- How can you coordinate the work of specialists in ways that extend opportunities and preserve the curriculum?
- How can you make best use of specialists who can be resources for my professional learning?

We have been increasingly committed to making grade-level instruction (the shared reading, interactive read-alouds, and writing instruction we described in Chapter 6) the lifeblood of curriculum and instruction. We have also seen many examples of schools where that instruction is conducted in a setting not unlike a train station—adults and students pulled out and pushed back in willy-nilly. Figure 8.1 presents the conundrum. In this chapter, we will advocate for classroom teachers as team captains and provide you with ideas for coordinating the work of other adults with your own.

Understanding the Roles of Specialists in Your School
. . . .

Here's the short version. Specialists work for you. You don't work for them. Specialists are there to help you ensure that your students get a deeper, broader experience in school. In schools with weak leadership, sometimes specialists (whom we

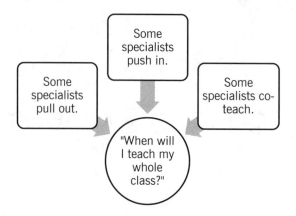

FIGURE 8.1. Challenges of coordinating the work of a team.

define as adults whose roles are specified and do not include primary responsibility for grade-level standards-based ELA instruction) seem to rule the roost. We'll start by identifying the specialists with whom you might work and specifying their roles. As you read about specialists, we wonder how many of you will be thinking about master's programs. We hope some of you will; we need specialists who begin in classroom teaching and then choose areas of real interest and talent. We also know that others will lament the fact that their school doesn't have these professionals. Remember, though, that the hiring of specialists nearly always increases class size.

• *School nurses* coordinate care between medical professionals, schools, and homes. They manage crises at schools involving sickness and injury, and they coordinate resources for students with chronic health conditions. They identify physical and mental health challenges that interfere with learning (Mcintosh, Thomas, & Maughan, 2015).

• *Art, music, and physical education teachers* are responsible for one and only one subject area. They study development and instruction across grade levels, and usually design a vertically articulated program, teaching all children in a school once per week. Because of the nature of the curriculum and the equipment children need, they typically have their own space and teachers bring children to work with them.

• *Instructional paraprofessionals* are adults who work with children but do no lesson planning. They use lesson plans written by teachers or specialists, or they use scripted commercial plans. They typically have no time during the day for preparation. In schools with Title I funds, the U.S. Department of Education requires paraprofessionals to have attended 2 years of college, earned at least an associate's degree, and met a state standard for demonstrating knowledge of reading, writing, and math.

- *Apprentice teachers*, or student teachers, are individuals seeking initial licensure who are doing an extended practicum in an authentic educational setting. Increasingly, these apprentice teachers are called co-teachers, although there is an important distinction. Apprentice teachers are mentored by master teachers, and the apprentice's responsibility for planning and implementing instruction increases over time. Currently, in most states, apprentice teachers do not replace classroom teachers; they work with them. In all cases, master teachers have a supervisory role for the apprentice and are alone responsible for student achievement (Friend, Embury, & Clarke, 2015).

- *Co-teachers*, or *inclusion teachers*, are credentialed professionals who team with regular education teachers to provide collaborative services to students with disabilities or students learning English as a second language for all or part of the instructional day. Both individuals are equally responsible for planning and providing instruction; both are equally responsible for student achievement. These teachers must operate as professional equals (Friend, Embury, & Clarke, 2015).

- *Special educators* are teachers with additional training in individualizing educational and behavior supports, in connecting with families, and in accommodating or modifying the curriculum to maximize individual students' learning opportunities. Special educators operate by pushing into classrooms, pulling children out of classrooms, or replacing classroom instruction with self-contained instruction. Special educators' write and enact IEPs, including measurable performance goals for students with disabilities of all types (Council for Exceptional Children, 2013).

- *English as a second language (ESL) specialists* possess expertise in oral language acquisition. They understand the cultural and linguistic characteristics of children's home environments; they understand the development of English language speaking and listening proficiency. ESL specialists may operate by pushing in to a classroom to provide services, by pulling children out of a classroom, or by co-teaching.

- *Gifted and talented education (GATE) specialists* are education professionals charged with identifying and providing broad and specialized curriculum experiences for children who display above-average ability, high levels of task commitment, and high levels of creativity (Young & Balli, 2014). GATE specialists typically take children out of the classroom for services.

- *School library media specialists* manage day-to-day operations in the school's media center and purchase both print and electronic resources, but their professional standards make it clear that they can do much more. They teach library and research skills to children, partner with teachers to design instruction including texts and/or technology, serve as information specialists, and administer programs with their own budgets (Cooper & Bray, 2011).

• *Instructional technology specialists* typically have dual roles, attending both to the design and maintenance of technology networks and to co-teaching and co-planning to support teachers and students who are learning to work with technology (Johnston, 2015).

• *Reading specialists* are responsible for supporting reading achievement in general and for serving struggling readers directly through interventions. They have specialized training in assessment and instruction. They can administer and interpret formal and informal assessments to identify student needs and design or deliver specialized instruction. They are also responsible for taking on leadership roles in the design of the literacy curriculum (Board of Directors, International Reading Association, 2000). We only consider individuals with master's degrees in reading or literacy education to be reading specialists.

• *Coaches* are different from reading specialists, although their credentials are often the same. Coaches work mainly with teachers, and they engage in activities at varying levels of intensity. Low-intensity coaching activities include hands-on support of the work of classroom teachers—administering assessments, working on curriculum projects, and engaging in group and individual problem solving. Moderate-intensity activities include co-planning, providing professional learning, facilitating team meetings, and interpreting assessment data. High-intensity activities include co-teaching, modeling, observation, and feedback. Coaches provide support for teachers and do not participate in teacher evaluation (Board of Directors, International Reading Association, 2004).

• *Speech–language pathologists* specialize in communication (speaking and listening) disorders and diagnose a very broad range of such disorders. They typically operate as part of a school's special education service team, and they can provide intervention directly, collaborate or consult with other professionals, or supervise paraprofessionals who offer services. They are increasingly charged with connecting their interventions to the classroom curriculum (Harn, Bradshaw, & Ogletree, 1999).

• *Occupational therapists* help individuals participate fully in everyday activities. They provide evaluations and design individual interventions and evaluation plans. They also help identify adaptive equipment that could make participation in a school environment more productive for an individual with a physical disability.

• *School psychologists* have advanced degrees ranging from master's to specialist to doctoral degrees. Their professional training includes data-based decision making and accountability; consultation and collaboration; interventions and instructional support to develop academic skills; interventions and mental health services to develop social and life skills; schoolwide practices to promote learning; preventive and responsive services; family–school collaboration services; diversity in development and learning; research and program evaluation; and legal, ethical, and professional practice issues. They typically take an active role in the IEP process, including conducting classroom observations. Often an individual school psychologist will serve multiple schools.

Judging How Specialists Are Scheduled

In the descriptions above, specialists provide an embarrassment of riches. While some very specialized services can only be provided at a set day and time, in most cases a well-informed classroom teacher can coordinate most services so that they supplement rather than supplant the curriculum. To supplant means supersede and replace. Too often, we forget to advocate for a school day during which each minute is scheduled for a particular teaching and learning goal. It is our view that when a student misses a part of the day's instruction for a particular service or opportunity, that instruction must be delivered as part of the service the student receives. The trick is to associate each specialist consistently with a part of your curriculum so that, as much as possible, the specialists supplement rather than supplant what you are doing.

Here are some examples: If GATE teachers offer services to children identified for giftedness three time per week, during science instruction, GATE services should meet (and exceed) the science goals that week. ELL services might replace an interactive read-aloud and writing for 45 minutes each day, but they should use the teacher's selected text and writing genre as part of their service plan. If reading specialists, special educators, or instructional paraprofessionals can come into the classroom for one period each day, it makes the most sense for that period to be the one when the classroom teacher is providing differentiated instruction. The services of those professionals can supplant or supplement what the teacher would have been able to do alone. In a supplanting model, the specialist provides a different type or quantity of intervention, as long as the intervention is more intense and more individualized than what the teacher would have been able to provide. In a supplemental model, the teacher first provides differentiation and the specialist provides a second dose of intervention to replace student self-selected reading. It is important to know the difference and to advocate that each student receives all parts of the curriculum, regardless of who provides them.

The key to all of this is scheduling. To make it work, teachers have to schedule their instructional day so that particular parts of the curriculum are staggered across the entire school day. If all teachers teach math or science first thing in the morning, a GATE specialist cannot supplant that curriculum with a more specialized one across all grade levels. If all teachers teach ELA in the morning,

	Classroom 1	Classroom 2	Classroom 3
45 minutes	Differentiation with Specialists	Shared Reading	Read-Aloud and Writing
45 minutes	Read-Aloud and Writing	Differentiation with Specialists	Shared Reading
45 minutes	Shared Reading	Read-Aloud and Writing	Differentiation with Specialists

FIGURE 8.2. Staggered ELA block to coordinate the work of specialists.

an intervention team cannot push in to supplement or supplant classroom-based differentiation. It's a trade-off. Figure 8.2 provides a simple example of staggered ELA times for a three-classroom grade-level team. You will see that no two parts of the curriculum occur at the same time; specialists could supplement or supplant the same part of the curriculum in all three classrooms.

Remember that we broke the school day into eight 45-minute blocks with 30 minutes left over. If classroom teams adopt a staggered schedule across the whole day, the system becomes even more organized. Figure 8.3 distributes content areas over time during the day so that they do not overlap across grades. While you may not be responsible for the overall school schedule, providing administrators with models for using time wisely can help to coordinate the work of the team of professionals who are serving your students. It can also help you to understand why it is worth it to accept a schedule with specialists or lunch at times you do not prefer.

	Kindergarten	First Grade	Second Grade
15 minutes	Morning Routines		
Block 1	ELA	Math	Specials
Block 2	ELA	Math	Math
Block 3	ELA	Recess/Lunch	Math
Block 4	Recess/Lunch	ELA	Science or Social Studies
Block 5	Math	ELA	Recess/Lunch
Block 6	Math	ELA	ELA
Block 7	Specials	Science or Social Studies	ELA
Block 8	Science or Social Studies	Specials	ELA
15 minutes	Afternoon Routines		

FIGURE 8.3. Staggered content-area instruction to coordinate the work of specialists.

Reexamining How You Collaborate with Specialists

Given the complexity and variety of the adult presence in classrooms, it may surprise you to know that researchers study collaborations. Collaboration is about choice and commitment, and it takes many potential forms. As we have examined the professional literature on collaboration, we have realized that classroom teachers must build many different kinds of collaborative relationships with the members of their instructional team. It may be helpful for you to see your choices. Pawan and Ortloff (2011) considered six different models of collaboration. They are listed and defined in Figure 8.4.

Here, an ounce of prevention is worth a pound of cure. We believe that you should begin using a shared decision-making model to set your classroom instructional schedule and that you advocate for staggering within and across grade levels. Once your personal schedule is set, you should identify all of the specialists with whom you will be collaborating. Your specialists include any intervention providers (e.g., instructional paraprofessionals, reading teachers, ESL teachers) assigned to support you. They include any members of the special education service team (special educators, speech language pathologists, occupational therapists, GATE specialists) identified in the IEPs of your students with disabilities or those identified for gifted education services. Finally, you should identify any individuals with whom you can co-plan or co-teach. Once you have a full list of people providing services to your children, your task is to engage in a second round of shared decision making to set the times and places (inside or outside your classroom) that they will serve your students.

Once you know the whos, whens, and wheres, it is time to decide whether you will be sharing information, participating cooperatively, or transferring responsibility. What you want to avoid is agreeing to "make up" the curriculum that an

Model	Nature of Collaboration
Consultation	Partners seek information from one another.
Information Exchange	Partners each gather different types of information about students, but then they share it.
Shared Decision Making	Partners make decisions in a democratic way, discussing solutions to problems and aiming for consensus.
Cooperative Participation	Partners are equals, planning and teaching together.
Responsibility Transfer	One partner cedes responsibility to another for a specific aspect of teaching and learning.
Interagency Learning	Partners are members of different school communities, but come together to compare and contrast ideas.

FIGURE 8.4. Potential collaboration models.

individual misses when receiving services from a specialist. For those specialists who conduct assessments, make sure they have a plan for sharing information. For those who will be co-teaching, make sure that you have a time and structure for participating cooperatively in planning and providing instruction. For those who will be assisting you during differentiation, decide whether they will be supplanting your intervention (requiring you to engage in responsibility transfer) or supplementing it (requiring that you engage in information sharing).

Not all specialists will be willing or able to schedule their time so that it fits your instructional schedule. In all cases, you will have to act as a case manager so that you can keep parents and others at school informed about the whole picture of your children's experiences in school. The following list provides discussion starters to engage those professionals in collaborations that maintain a focus on your students and what they need.

- "You want to come on _____ at _____. During that time, I will be teaching _____. Can you think of any ways that you can include that content while you accomplish your goals?"
- "Help me understand how you set your goals and how you will see if they are met."
- "Are there ways that I can use what you are doing at other times of day?"
- "What is the easiest way for us to communicate about progress and problems?"
- "_____ is also working with _____. Can we set up a way to communicate so that all of us get the information we need?"

Rethinking How You Collaborate with Peers

In general, your collaborations with specialists are about coordinating services for your students. Other collaborations are about accomplishing your own work. Your most potentially productive and timesaving collaborations will be with your peers—the teachers who are co-teaching with you and those who are also teaching at your grade level. We urge you to collaborate with them from four angles and in this order: exchange information, share decision making, transfer responsibility, and participate cooperatively. Figure 8.5 provides a visual of the process.

All teachers know (or learn quickly) that curriculum materials and standards do not a coherent plan make. The real work comes when we use standards to decide exactly when, why, and how to use available materials. That is a task for which several heads are better than one. It is a perfect opportunity for collaborations that save time and work. It makes sense to begin with a free information exchange, with team members sharing insights into the demands of the standards and the opportunities provided by curriculum materials. After a free exchange, the

Exchange information.	Share decision making.	Transfer responsibility.	Participate collaboratively.
• Discuss standards and curriculum resources.	• Decide on instructional frames and routines.	• Divide responsibility for lesson planning.	• Deliver instruction as equals with co-teachers.

FIGURE 8.5. Process for collaborating with peers.

discussion must turn to decision making, with team members sharing the responsibility for choosing an overall framework for how time and materials will be used. As you saw in Chapter 6, we favor a daily routine for each part of the ELA block (shared reading, differentiated instruction, and interactive read-alouds or writing), but you may be more comfortable with a weekly routine. If you have come to consensus on the overall framework for planning an instructional week, four team members can plan one week each to accomplish a month's planning—but only if you are willing to relinquish control and trust your colleagues. With a month's planning work accomplished, it is much easier to decide how to divide and provide the instruction with any co-teaching partners.

Grouping for Instruction

While grade-level instruction can be planned collaboratively with only standards and curriculum materials, differentiation must also rely on student-level data. We have been working with school-level and grade-level teams to move from an "I differentiate" to a "we differentiate" model, again distributing the work and the responsibility for decision making.

First, we want to be clear about what we mean by grouping for instruction. We support the formation of homeroom classes that comprise a range of achievement. Once data are available for most students, after the kindergarten year, we think that all classes should begin with relatively similar numbers of high-, average-, and low-achieving learners. The alternative, ability grouping or tracking, places students with similar abilities together in homeroom classes. Data suggest that during the first years of school, this practice results in substantially weaker gains for the lowest-achieving students and only slightly larger gains for the highest-achieving students. Over the long term, this tiny initial advantage in learning trajectory for initially high achievers does not justify the costs to initially low achievers (Lleras & Rangel, 2009). On balance, we view ability grouping at the classroom level as an inequitable educational practice.

When teachers support grouping, they may do so not from a student equity stance but from a planning and management position. There is no doubt that planning for differentiation is more complex if your student achievement is more diverse. But there is a middle ground, we think, if you are willing to collaborate with your peers. Our experience with grouping students for differentiated instruction within a classroom typically reveals that a large majority (more than 85% of a class) can be taught in three groups. We view that as a manageable system, especially if the school's differentiation model (e.g., our skill-based model or guided reading) is clear.

What makes differentiation difficult is the few students who are actually higher-achieving than the rest of the children in the highest group and those few who are actually lower-achieving than the rest of the children in the lowest group. There are two solutions to this common problem. The first is the use of specialists who come into the classroom during differentiation time when schools stagger parts of ELA instruction, as in Figure 8.2. Classroom teachers should feel confident transferring responsibility for differentiation to specialists who are part of their instructional team. That may be the best way for the teacher to provide these students with what they need; the teacher is ensuring that the students with the most needs have the most intense instruction possible. When a classroom teacher makes that choice, he or she is advocating for students—not abandoning them.

Not all schools will have specialists push in during instruction. This is where collaboration with grade-level teammates can help. If teammates determine up front that all children will receive 15 minutes of differentiated instruction, and they have a 45-minute differentiation block, that means that the total number of possible groups is the number of team members multiplied by 3. Perhaps with the support of a reading specialist or coach, a grade-level team can look at data and distribute students among the groups, striving to maximize the homogeneity of groups rather than to control their size. Teachers can then reflect on their own instructional strengths and take responsibility for teaching the groups they believe they can serve best. This within-grade-level grouping system, often called a "walk to read" system, ensures that no teacher will have more than three differentiation groups and that all children will have the chance to be placed in an appropriate group.

Sharing Grade-Level Data

Sometimes the highest-risk collaborations with peers provide the greatest opportunities. Again, we urge you to move from "me" to "we"—to be willing to bring your students' work to the table, to ask your colleagues to help you interpret it, and to look for trends that can guide improvements. This is risky because sometimes you will notice that your students' achievement is weaker than that of another team member. We see this as a golden opportunity to collaborate. Remember: You are not in competition with your teammates. All of you are together in competition with standards. Everyone wins when you are willing to admit weaknesses and seek help from colleagues with different strengths.

One place where many teachers are building knowledge is in the area of writing. Writing is a good place to share grade-level data, especially because the data are so transparent. Writing in the early primary years requires handwriting, spelling, and composition. If you and your colleagues agree to assign the same writing prompt, you can easily compare and contrast on those three traits. In each area, you may find that achievement within all classes is very diverse. You will be lucky, though, if you find one classroom where achievement in any one area is visibly better. That will allow you to explore potential explanations. Are there instructional routines that this person is using that you are not? Does feedback differ? Are specialists or instructional paraprofessionals helping in different ways? Shared classroom-level data should be a source of strength and collegiality. Data should help build relationships and be a driving force behind a grade-level professional learning community.

Summary

Schools are complex organizations. Classroom teachers find themselves at the center of a sometimes-large team of peers, assistants, and specialists. They must understand the roles of these additional team members and be willing to collaborate with them. What they can't afford to do, though, is let specialists rule the roost. We believe that grade-level instruction, provided to groups of children heterogeneous by achievement, should be protected from interruption. We believe that teachers can accomplish this goal if they are careful and collaborative in setting their daily schedules, if they consider models that supplement and models that supplant particular segments of instruction, and if they are willing to collaborate with their grade-level peers.

CHAPTER 9

Organizing Your Children's Books

- How many books should be available in a primary or preschool classroom?
- What kinds of books should be available?
- How can you fill the gaps you identify in your classroom library?
- How are the kinds of books linked to instructional purposes?
- What are effective ways of storing books?

In Chapter 5, we offered a broad view of the primary classroom environment and discussed a number of features other than books. We acknowledged, however, that books are the most important component of the classroom environment. When we walk into a classroom, the first things we notice are the type, amount, and organization of books. Given their importance, we now examine in more detail the books available to you as you teach. Our focus will be on both the nature of the books and how they are organized.

Judging the Quantity, Range, and Display of Available Books

Conducting an inventory of the tradebooks available in a primary classroom is a useful first step in evaluating your needs. Hoffman et al. (2004), in their TEX-IN3 instrument, offer a research-based guide to help researchers (and teachers) do exactly that. Altogether, it allows an observer to appraise three dimensions of a classroom's texts: (1) an inventory of quality and variety, (2) the use of books by teachers, and (3) interviews of the teacher and students. In this chapter, our focus is on the text environment only, and we have included an additional portion of the TEX-IN3 (Hoffman et al., 2004).

Two rubrics allow you to take stock of the text environment of your classroom. The first is designed to appraise a number of dimensions, including the range, quantity, appeal, organization, and accessibility of books. Each element of the rubric involves rating on a 1–5 scale. The tradebook rubric appears in Figure 9.1. (Note that only points 1, 3, and 5 are formally described.)

Judging the Overall Text Environment

Figure 9.2 affords a broader take on the literacy environment. Its main focus is on tradebooks, but local texts are also included. Note that its five ratings correspond to those used for local texts in Figure 6.3. We agree with Hoffman and his colleagues that it is important to think of books and local texts together as inseparable components of a productive literacy environment.

You Know Where Everything Is—So Why Organize?

In a spirit of full disclosure, we often raise this question about our offices. The unfortunate result is that we often cannot locate items without a good deal of searching. Unless we're pressed to meet a deadline, these searches can be merely annoying. In classroom contexts, however, they can result in lost instructional time and even management issues. Although this is surely reason enough to keep books and other materials organized, there is another consideration as well. Children must be able to locate appropriate books and materials whenever they need them.

Storing Books in a Primary Classroom

As you organize the books in your classroom, you should keep two questions foremost in mind: Who will use them and for what purpose? Some books only you will need to find, such as big books used for shared or fingerpoint reading. These should be stored in two places, a more or less permanent place and a second, temporary place that is near your easel. You can rotate books in and out of the active area.

Dimension	1. Inadequate	3. Basic	5. Outstanding
Quantity/ Variety	• The classroom contains between one and seven books per child in the classroom collection. • Less than 10% of the collection is non-narrative. • Less than 30% of the books have been published in the past 3 years. • There is an absence of some type of tradebooks or an extreme imbalance in the numbers available. • Multiple copies of texts are not included.	• Between 8 and 19 books per child in the classroom collection. • Between 10 and 20% of the collection is non-narrative. • Between 30 and 50% of the books have been published in the past 3 years. • Picture books, easy chapter books, and challenge books are available, but the proportion is not matched to student needs and interests. • Multiple copies of a few of the texts are available.	• More than 20 books per child in the classroom collection. More than 20% of the collection is non-narrative. • More than 50% of the books have been published in the past 3 years. • There is a balance of picture, easy chapter, and challenge books available. • Multiple copies of many texts are available. Student-authored books may be included.
Engaging Qualities (language, design, content)	• The collection is severely limited in terms of books that are rich in language and design. • The content is narrow and not motivating to the full range of developmental levels of the students in this class.	• The majority of the collection can be characterized in terms of rich language, rich design, and content that is varied and motivating to the full range of developmental levels of the students in this class.	• The collection can be characterized in terms of rich language, rich design, and content that is varied and motivating to the full range of developmental levels of the students in this class.
Accessibility (display, organization)	• The books are not displayed in the classroom in a particularly attractive manner. • Texts are restricted to a central library section of the class that is not prominent. • The texts are displayed in a manner that severely restricts access by the students. There is no apparent organizational plan for the texts that support student use.	• The books are displayed in an attractive manner. • Texts tend to be located in a central library section of the class. • The texts are displayed in a manner that provides for easy access by the students. • The texts are organized in a simple manner that facilitates student ease of use.	• The texts are displayed in the classroom in a highly attractive and thoughtful manner. • The texts are located around the classroom in connection to content. • The texts are displayed in a manner that actively encourages student engagement. • The texts are organized in a variety of ways that facilitate student ease of use (e.g., by authors, by types, by content).
Challenge Level (decodability, predictability, and vocabulary load)	• The books don't match well with the range of abilities and skills of the class. • The books tend to be either too hard or too easy for most of the students. • There is little available for those at the extremes.	• The books are well suited to the average level of students in the class in terms of challenge and support levels (decodability, predictability, and vocabulary). • The choices for struggling or accelerated readers are limited.	• The books offer a wide range of challenge and support levels (decodability, predictability, and vocabulary).

FIGURE 9.1. TEX-IN3 rubric for tradebooks. From Hoffman, Sailors, Duffy, and Beretvas (2004). Copyright 2004 by Sage Publications. All rights reserved.

5. **Extremely rich.** The text environment is an extremely rich resource for students. The quantity of texts available and the range of text types are extensive. Obvious care has been given to the careful selection of texts that fit the range of students' diverse needs and interests. The texts represent a wide range of cultural perspectives and include languages other than English. These texts link in obvious ways to the curriculum not only in reading and the language arts, but also across the content areas. Local texts are plentiful in the classroom at both the personal and the public levels. The texts reflect uses of literacy that are functional to the daily life in the classroom.

4. **Rich.** The text environment provides a rich resource for the vast majority of students. The quantity and range of texts are more than adequate for the needs of the class. There are texts that represent various cultures and might include languages other than English to meet the range of diverse needs of students. The text environment may be exceptional in some areas (e.g., the range and number of tradebook literature available for the students) and is only adequate in others (e.g., the availability and display of expository texts). Local texts are clearly valued in this classroom, although commercial texts are more apparent. Student input into the creation of the text environment is clearly evidenced (e.g., student-authored texts, displays, charts).

3. **Functional.** The text environment is functional as a resource for most students. The supply is adequate and the range of texts, though limited, is present. The texts show little evidence of cultural or linguistic diversity. Commercial texts dominate. Narrative texts dominate in the trade literature available. Some expository texts are available, but the number, appropriateness, and quality are limited. The texts in the classroom may appear organized, but there is little sense of an underlying design for the text environment that will be engaging for and used by the students. There is some evidence of student involvement in the creation of the text environment.

2. **Limited.** The text environment is limited. Texts are available; however, they tend to be of mediocre quality and are directed toward the on-grade level reader in the class. Few texts are available that meet the needs of struggling or highly skilled readers. Commercial texts dominate in the classroom. The collection suggests whole-class use of texts, 1 with small text sets or individual titles limited. Local texts may be available but are of poor quality and do not appear accessible or functional. Little apparent attention has been given to the display or the organization of the texts in the classroom. Student input into the text environment is limited to Work Product Displays.

1. **Inadequate.** The text environment is severely limited and cannot be regarded as a meaningful resource for the vast majority of children. Few, if any, local texts are present. Even the few commercial texts available tend to be of low quality. Restrictive worksheets and workbooks characterize the personal texts available for student use. There is little evidence of student input into the text environment.

FIGURE 9.2. TEX-IN3 rubric for the holistic text environment. From Hoffman, Sailors, Duffy, and Beretvas (2004). Copyright 2004 by Sage Publications. All rights reserved.

Most of the books in your classroom will be accessed by students, which means that you must be careful to make their organization visual. There are several ways to house books so that they are readily accessible to children. By far the most efficient method is to place them on shelves with the spines facing out. If you have the luxury of a large number of books, you will no doubt need to shelve them in this way, but doing so has drawbacks. Cover art, cleverly created to lure readers, is concealed.

This is also a problem with several other means of storing books, such as tubs, crates, and stacked cubbies. In each case, children must sort through books one at a time to make a judgment. Using open-faced shelves or the marker tray to display the covers of books is a way around this, but only a limited number can be shown in this manner (see Figure 9.3). Using a featured book approach and rotating those in view at any given time is a compromise solution.

We should add that wire racks (stationary or swivel) are another means of displaying books with their covers displayed. These are popular in the upper grades, but in the primary classroom a teacher must think about the room they take up, whether they are sufficiently stable, and whether the highest books are within reach.

FIGURE 9.3. Open-faced shelving used to reveal cover art.

Approaches to Organizing

There are many ways of organizing your tradebooks so that you and your children can more easily access them. The best approach is to begin with features that are likely to be the most useful. These include level of difficulty, topic or theme, and genre. Organizing books by two of these categories is easy. For example, the shelves depicted in Figure 9.4 show how books might be organized by level of difficulty and genre at the same time. Adding a third category can be a bit tricky, but there are ways to do it.

Organizing by Level

Imagine a tub filled with a random assortment of trade books. At first, it might seem simple to arrange them in linear fashion from the easiest to the most difficult. In reality, the process is not so straightforward. It is based on compromises and estimates at every step of the way. To begin with, the Lexile (the main metric used to gauge text complexity) is not particularly useful below grade 2. You may already use the lettering system associated with guided reading, but this approach is imprecise and depends on more than the text itself (e.g., illustrations and topic). We are not suggesting that there is no validity to such approaches. We are merely pointing out that they involve approximations.

Vertical dividers, such as those shown in Figure 9.5, can be useful in grouping the books by general difficulty level. The shelving system might also consist of

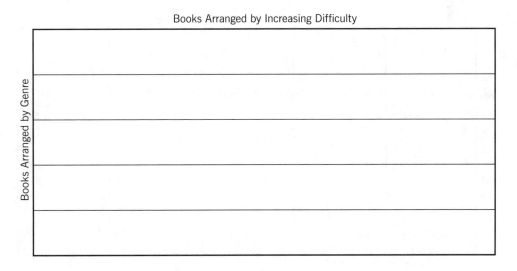

FIGURE 9.4. Organizational plan for shelved tradebooks.

stacked cubbies, so the dividers are actually the sides of each cubby. Notice that dividers enable you and your students to sort through a great many books quickly and systematically to find the desirable ones based on two characteristics, difficulty and genre. This rectangular system has a hidden benefit as well. It lends itself to teachable moments as you explain how such a system works. The transfer of this idea to charts is an easy one.

Organizing by Genre

The word *genre* has several meanings, but in the primary grades we think it best to take a broad approach, separating books into literature and information texts. It is also useful to separate information books into science and social studies. We have found that most nonfiction is primarily associated with one of these two broad fields. And in most of the classroom libraries we visit, the number of available titles is comparable in these two areas. The same is not true for literature. If we use fiction and poetry as a means of categorizing them, we will almost undoubtedly have far more fiction titles. We can address this problem by marking the books with stickers or using some other simple method.

Because a balance between literature and information books is often lacking in the primary grades (Duke, 2000, 2003), we have devoted two shelves to each as a visual reminder of where you stand. Figure 9.6 shows how this arrangement might appear.

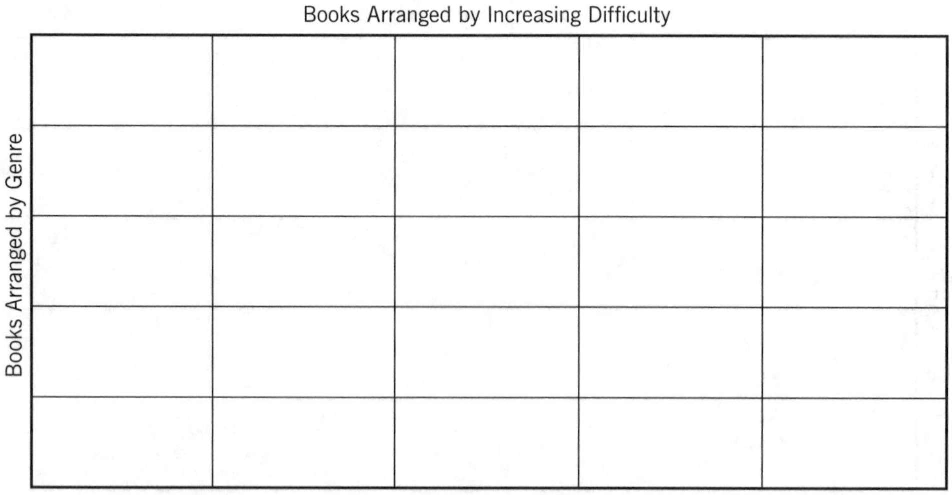

Books Arranged by Increasing Difficulty

Books Arranged by Genre

FIGURE 9.5. Vertical dividers help to classify books by difficulty.

Books Arranged by Increasing Difficulty

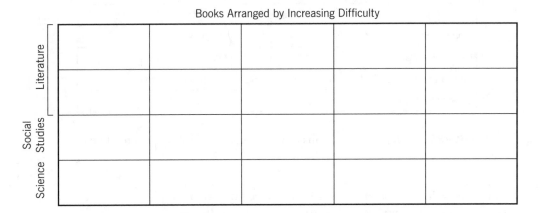

FIGURE 9.6. Shelving system that reflects important features of tradebooks.

Organizing by Topic or Theme

Up to this point, our shelving system is arranged as follows. Books are organized by difficulty from left to right. The top two shelves are devoted to literature, fiction and poetry combined. The third and fourth shelves are devoted to social studies and science nonfiction. How does our proposed system accommodate topics and themes, such as life in colonial America or how to contend with fear? The problem is that various themes might occur in books located on any of the shelves and at almost any difficulty level, but if you were to reorganize your books by theme, you would need to give up the pattern we have already established. But there is a better way!

Inventorying Your Books

The important idea is to know which books you have so that you can plan around them, pull them easily, and temporarily store them in a separate location. A simple database in which books are tagged by theme or topic can help you do this without the necessity of permanently rearranging the books themselves.

Benefits of Excel

A good way to accomplish this goal is by maintaining an Excel file that lists all the books in your room together with several key features. Figure 9.7 presents part of a sample Excel file with a few titles that a second-grade teacher has entered along with several key features. These include the Lexile, the genre, and the predominant

Title	Lexile	Genre	Topic	Standard
Magnets Push, Magnets Pull	740	S	Magnets	
How a Plant Grows	590	S	Plants	
Amelia and Eleanor Go for a Ride	600	SS	American Women	
Gooney Bird Greene	590	F	Humor	

FIGURE 9.7. Simple Excel database used to categorize classroom textbooks.

theme. These last two features are coded according to a simple system the teacher has decided to use. In this case, genre is coded as follows:

- F = fiction
- P = poetry
- SS = social studies informational books
- S = science informational books

A coding system for themes or topics will be more extensive, of course, and will depend on the books available. Here, the teacher has used one-word tags to indicate the theme or topic. It is also a good idea to categorize by standard, especially in the case of science and social studies.

Setting up an Excel file of this sort might require a few hours, but the benefits can be enormous. This is because the teacher is in a position to sort the books according to one or more features. For example, a list of all books dealing with important American women and written within a given difficulty range can easily be generated. The work of constructing a database of this sort can be shared among teachers, provided their classrooms are equipped with largely similar libraries.

You can tell that we are not digital natives. Of course, if you are, there is an app for that. Search apps for bookshelves or for keeping track of music libraries. They typically allow you to scan the books' barcodes and ISBN numbers to access and store titles and authors. Then you can add additional information. Search bookshelf apps to see your choices.

Filling Gaps

You can initially size up the collection of tradebooks in your classroom library by examining gaps that become apparent through your shelving system. For example, it may become clear that you have very few science books written at a low level of text complexity. A more detailed method of determining where gaps exist, however, is the database you have created. Sorting by topic will alert you to the need for additional books. Sorting by science or social studies standards may identify important gaps as well.

Finally, consider adding an additional column for the location of the book. A given title may be located in a colleague's room but not in yours (another benefit of collaboration). Moreover, the school library might house additional titles of a given type, and tagging them by location can help you find them. Here, the library media specialist can be your best friend.

Summary

Organizing the books in your room is important for many reasons. It saves time, it allows you to pull books for particular purposes, and it helps you identify gaps. Straightforward rubrics can help you judge the quantity, range, and appeal of the books available to you and your students. They can also provide an idea of the overall literacy environment of your classroom when they are combined with the rubrics for other features of that environment, such as local text displays.

The books that are intended to be used by children can be organized by difficulty level, genre, and topic or theme. Because a balance of literature and information books is desirable in every primary classroom, a shelving system that separates books in this manner can be revealing.

A database consisting of a simple Excel file can also help in identifying gaps, pulling titles together temporarily for a particular purpose, and ensuring that content standards are addressed. When such a database is extended to include books located in other classrooms and in the school media center, the result is a powerful tool indeed.

CHAPTER 10

. . . .

Establishing Routines

GUIDING QUESTIONS

• Why are classroom routines essential in the early primary classroom?

• How can you build routines that enhance children's instructional opportunities?

• How can you build routines that help children to make transitions between activities?

• How can you manage disruptions in a positive manner?

Understanding the Importance of Routines

All teachers, even apprentice teachers, will say that classroom management is important, and many will say that they worry about it. The phrase *classroom management* has a negative connotation to us. We prefer the term *classroom routines*, and we will discuss routines within and between segments of the curriculum. Routines are repeated procedures that can be planned and taught and learned and used.

We have entered many early primary classrooms and seen nearly invisible routines and total student comfort and engagement. It is tempting to think that the teachers in those classrooms are just "born" teachers, but we know that they are not. What they have in common is a commitment to setting the stage for learning *before* they begin the nuts and bolts of teaching. They prevent disruptions by repeating the class norms every day, at every transition. They use auditory and physical signals. They have strong personal relationships with children and their families. The problem for us (and for teachers who are struggling to correct management problems) is that we were not there on the very first day of school. It's all about setting up and then teaching routines. Researchers who study classroom management (e.g., Jones, Bailey, & Jacob, 2014) have distilled four constant principles. Figure 10.1 presents them as a cycle because each influences another in turn.

Proactive classroom management is a mantra that all teachers hear preached, but the song sung by administrators and mentors is sometimes too vague. Sometimes it is accompanied by mention of "these kids," with the connotation that management problems are there because of weak parenting. Especially in the preschool and early primary years, self-regulation skills must be considered a normal instructional target for school, rather than a problem from home. Social and emotional learning is simply a type of learning like any other, one to be considered carefully by teachers and monitored over time. It is not a matter of teaching children to adapt to you and your expectations or to respect the authority of teachers. It is about teaching children to manage themselves.

Oftentimes schools adopt positive behavior support (PBS) systems that serve to link routines and cues across contexts. We support this general approach but must stop short of recommending specific PBS protocols. That is because we think that any schoolwide PBS system can be very helpful, but it is also up to individual teachers to implement it well and to reflect on its effects.

Teaching Instructional Routines

A classic study of effective first-grade teachers (Brophy, 1986) revealed that they actively established instructional routines. The good news is that all teachers can

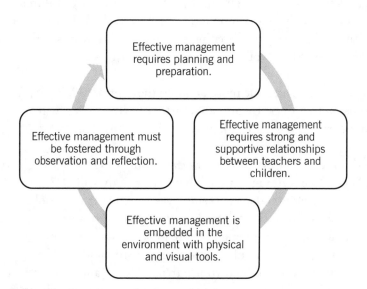

FIGURE 10.1. Principles of effective classroom management.

:ome more effective in the process. It may not be immediately appar-
tructional routines require specific skills that can be actively taught.
.. ue for adults as well as children. We have learned over time that coaching
teachers to use new instructional routines requires a very specific description of
what that new routine actually requires. Figure 10.2 presents a coaching form for
dialogic reading, which you will remember as the cornerstone of shared reading
in preschool and kindergarten. We typically design these forms as part of professional learning; we find that when we are specific about what we are trying to
teach teachers to do, we can actually teach it more quickly and effectively.

The same system might work well for you. For each of the instructional routines that you will use each day, first describe it exactly, with a set of required
characteristics at full implementation. While you are doing this, you will actually
be making a carefully tailored observation form for an administrator or coach
coming to observe you. Then it will be easier to plan how to teach your children to
engage in that routine. We favor a combination of direct explanation and physical
practice. For dialogic reading, then, you might consider teacher talk that is this
explicit:

"We are going to share a story every day. I am going to be the one reading
the story. When I am talking, you will have your body still, your hands still,
your listening ears ready, and your seeing eyes looking at the book. Let's practice getting ready to listen. Check to see if your body is still, your hands are
still, your listening ears are ready and your seeing eyes are looking. I can
see that _____ is ready. I can see that _____ is ready. [You can read a few
pages and then initiate a self-check, ideally before any children are actually
not listening.] Let's take a minute to check ourselves. Is your body still? Are
your hands still? Are your listening ears ready? Are your seeing eyes looking?
That's how you know you're ready to listen to this story."

On day 2, you can add one more detail to the routine. This time, you can teach
children to listen to a question and answer to a partner. That way no children are
waiting for a turn. Make your talk as repetitive as possible.

"We are going to share a story every day. I am going to be the one reading the
story. When I am talking, you will have your body still, your hands still, your
listening ears ready and your seeing eyes looking at the book. Let's practice
listening. Check to see if your body is still, your hands are still, your listening
ears are ready and your seeing eyes are looking. I can see that _____ is ready.
I can see that _____ is ready. Sometimes I'll stop and ask a question. When I
ask you to talk, you will hold your partner's hand and talk with your partner
in a quiet voice. When it's time to stop talking, I'll count down from 3–2–1.
When I get to 1, you'll stop your talk, let go of your partner's hand, and be

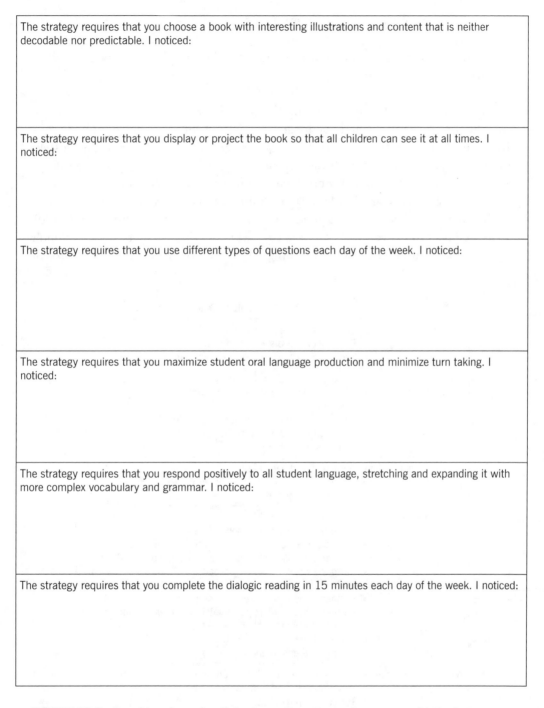

The strategy requires that you choose a book with interesting illustrations and content that is neither decodable nor predictable. I noticed:
The strategy requires that you display or project the book so that all children can see it at all times. I noticed:
The strategy requires that you use different types of questions each day of the week. I noticed:
The strategy requires that you maximize student oral language production and minimize turn taking. I noticed:
The strategy requires that you respond positively to all student language, stretching and expanding it with more complex vocabulary and grammar. I noticed:
The strategy requires that you complete the dialogic reading in 15 minutes each day of the week. I noticed:

FIGURE 10.2. Coaching form for dialogic reading. From *Organizing the Early Literacy Classroom: How to Plan for Success and Reach Your Goals* by Sharon Walpole and Michael C. McKenna. Copyright © 2016 The Guilford Press. Permission to photocopy this figure is granted to purchasers of this book for personal use or use with individual students (see copyright page for details). Purchasers can download enlarged versions of this figure (see the box at the end of the table of contents).

ν to listen again: Body still, hands still, listening ears ready and seeing eyes looking. Let's practice."

The trick to a really positive set of classroom instructional routines is that you take the time to think through what each step in that routine requires of your children. Then you have to set reasonable expectations of yourself to teach each step, adding new requirements each day. Some instructional routines take a week to teach; some take a month. All routines are simpler to teach as children get older, so we urge our preschool and kindergarten teammates to plan enough time to create a predictable, repetitive, instructional environment, and our first- and second-grade team members to expect more rapid mastery. Figure 10.3 presents some common instructional routines along with teaching targets. You can use the same approach

Routine	Skills to Teach
Sharing a Book	• Sit shoulder to shoulder. • Place book flat on desk between partners. • Each partner holds book open with outside hand. • Take turns turning pages.
Echo Reading	• Listen to teacher reading aloud while touching words. • Stop when teacher stops. • Move eyes and finger back to the beginning. • Touch and say words together with teacher. • Stop when teacher stops.
Choral Reading	• Get finger and eyes ready. • Touch and say words together with teacher. • Stop when teacher stops.
Partner Reading	• Sit shoulder to shoulder. • Place book flat on desk between partners. • Each partner holds book open with outside hand. • Partner 1 reads while partner 2 looks at words and listens. • Partner 1 asks for help if needed. • Partner 2 waits to be asked. • Partner 1 reads to the end of the page. • Partner 2 reads while partner 1 looks at words and listens. • Partner 2 asks for help if needed. • Partner 1 waits to be asked. • Partner 2 reads to end of the page.
Writing in a Journal	• Think about what you are supposed to draw or write. • Find the last page that you wrote on. • Turn to the next page. • Write your name at the top. • Copy the date at the top. • Draw a picture on the top. • Write about it on the bottom.

FIGURE 10.3. Components of instructional routines.

for other routines as well, by first breaking the procedure down into the steps you want students to follow.

Pace yourself! You can't teach all of these routines in a day. We tend to teach and (schedule) in manageable chunks. Maybe your goal for the first week will be to teach the morning check-in and the routines associated with your first 45-minute block. The rest of the day can be used for relationship building, with children sharing information about themselves and their families.

Teaching Transition Procedures

Lots can happen during transitions, and the quality of transitions seeps into the next instructional segment, either setting it up in a positive way or negatively coloring it. One of the reasons that transitions are difficult is that children do not want to leave tasks unfinished or to stop engaging in favorite tasks. Think about it. How often are people actually forced to start and stop work without first completing it? Plan for that by including directions about when unfinished work will be completed or when favorite tasks will be engaged in again.

We have seen fantastic transition routines. Often teachers give a two-minute warning to help students for whom transitions are very difficult. Many include music or lighting changes to signal transitions without speech. Most, especially for preschool and kindergarten children, include an attractive activity to make the transition itself something that children look forward to. We have seen Simon Says, yoga stretches, line dances, songs with movement, buddy systems—the choices are nearly endless. What they have in common is that the transition procedures themselves are enjoyable for all, and nearly always narrated by the teacher, who is calmly repeating the necessary steps *every day* so that children feel supported in what they need to do.

As with instructional routines, transition routines need to be defined, practiced, and then applied consistently. And they don't develop overnight:

"We are going to start our mornings with a story. I am going to pick the story and set it up over here. When I start the morning music, you will leave your morning work on your desk, stand up from your seat, push in your chair, and come and sit on your own square on the rug. Let's practice that first. There are five steps: Listen for the music, leave your morning work on your desk, stand up from your seat, push in your chair, and come and sit on your own square on the rug . . . That was a great start. Go back to your seats. Let's practice it again. Listen for the music, leave your morning work on your desk, stand up from your seat, push in your chair, and come and sit on your own square on the rug. I'll give you time later to finish your morning work. Right now we are going to share a great story."

Teaching Children to Complete Independent Work

One of the most challenging routines to teach is also the one that is most essential to meeting the varied needs of children. In order to meet with small groups and accomplish differentiated instruction, you first have to set the stage by engaging the rest of the children in meaningful work without you. For our youngest learners, this is a very difficult expectation, and one that must be carefully nurtured. We actually think that the ability to work productively on one's own is a cornerstone on which many future learning experiences are built. We urge you to begin to foster this skill set as soon as possible.

In preschool and in many kindergartens, children's independent learning is accomplished in centers. When you are teaching independent learning routines, it is helpful to think of them as specific types of opportunities rather than simply as places. Centers are places where children work with specific manipulatives and cooperate with and talk to other children. After preschool, in many classrooms, there are no centers. Instead, there are independent work routines that are used each day.

 We have found that it is important to build up independent work stamina, teaching one independent routine at a time, and gradually increasing the time that children are spending on it. First, you have to identify the routines that you will use. You might have alphabet or word work, book browsing, and writing as initial targets. Each of these targets has materials to get and put away, goals or directions, and strategies for getting help from other children. It is reasonable to begin with teaching how to get materials, to set a timer for 5 minutes of work time, and then to teach how to put away materials. The next day, reteach how to get materials, increase the work time to 6 minutes, and reteach how to put away materials. Once you have children comfortable working for 10 minutes, you can call an individual student for 10 minutes of assessment each day as you increase the total work time to 15 minutes.

Judging Your Instructional Routines

Once you have your routines running, it is time for self-study. There are several important questions to consider:

- "Am I able to maintain the routines I have set?"
- "Are my routines maximizing instructional time?"
- "Are my routines minimizing negative interactions with children?"

Maintaining Consistency

When your routines are up and running, it may be tempting to stop using them. We think this is a mistake in early primary classrooms. Routines forgotten by children tend to require that you stop instruction to give corrective feedback. Taking a few seconds from time to time to consistently (and calmly) review the routines required for each activity each day can take that possibility off the table for most children.

Remember that your routines are there to teach children to manage their own behavior in positive ways. Researchers have found that a simple checklist can help you continue to implement the routines you have set and taught (Oliver, Wehby, & Nelson, 2015). For us, the creation of that checklist also makes your routines concrete and transparent—first to you, but then potentially to other stakeholders. Imagine how much easier it would be for a substitute teacher to have both lesson plans and a simple checklist of routines that your children know and use. Also think about how such a checklist could help you describe your routines to parents. The time you spend creating a checklist will be time well spent.

Checklist of routines

Watching the Clock

After a month or so, it makes sense to collect some real-time data to see how much of the time you've planned for each segment of your curriculum (e.g., shared reading, interactive read-alouds and writing, or differentiation) is actually available to you. You can conduct your own investigation here, but you have to be willing to report accurately. We suggest that you start with your full instructional schedule. See Chapter 6 to remind you of the full day's content, but make a chart with your own start and end times and your plans for time in each subject. You might also add a column for some comments where you reflect on the quality of that particular segment of your day.

Remember that one reason for your instructional routines and for transitions is to make the day predictable and organized for your children. If you collect data for three days running, you will get a good sense of whether your transition routines are allowing your instructional focus to shift across the day. You will be able to see how many minutes are gobbled up by transitions, and then you will be able to judge whether these minutes are few enough.

Watching Your Talk

In the end, routines are there to maximize instructional time and provide a comfortable and predictable learning environment. They are meant to be proactive; they prevent problems. It makes sense to consider how much redirection you need to provide as part of your overall evaluation of your routines. As with your focus on whether you consistently use your own routines, and whether those routines maximize instructional time, a small amount of data collection can provide a good deal of information about whether your routines are associated with a positive classroom climate, with relatively few instances of corrective or negative interaction with children. This is best accomplished through audio recording an instructional segment and then making a frequency table:

- Select a part of the day to evaluate.
- Record that part.
- Listen to the recording and mark the number of positive or proactive statements you make and the number of negative or corrective statements you make.

There is no "correct" proportion, but listening to your talk and looking at it as a balance of positive and corrective statements can help you to reflect on whether the routines you are using are creating the classroom community you want.

Adjusting Routines When Necessary

If you have been proactive in the setting and teaching of routines, you will be able to adjust them when they are not working. We suggest that you discuss your concerns about routines with your children, explaining what specifically does not seem to be working. That way you will be providing a meaningful context to any changes that may be difficult for some children. You will be strengthening trusting relationships by explaining changes rather than springing them on children. It may be that students can help each other self-monitor when they know that a particular routine isn't working and what about it isn't working. For example, if you present an honest description of a transition routine that is taking too long, and tell children that it is making science instruction or math instruction or the read-aloud period too brief, children may be able to adjust their behavior before you consider altering the routine.

Contending with Disruptions

Sometimes disruptions are fairly systemic. You may find, for example, that a particular routine or time of day is problematic for a number of children. One way to be proactive is to realize that your classroom is a place whose organization is determined by you and can be changed by you. You must be willing to return to routines if they are not working (Epstein, Atkins, Cullinan, Kutash, & Weaver, 2008). You can rearrange your student seating. You can change the order in which you see small groups. You can facilitate sharing of materials by changing the way they are stored. Respond to systemic disruption by making changes to the environment or the schedule.

Other times you will see that specific times or routines trouble a single child. This is normal; the best-planned routines simply will not work with every child. It may be helpful to remember that and to view it as a normal part of your instructional duties. Perhaps the most important way to respond to disruption is to think about it later. While we know that nothing is simple during an episode of disruptive behavior, there are simple and powerful things you can do afterward. Most importantly, you have to step away and document the context in which the behavior was observed and also the contexts in which it is absent (Epstein et al., 2008). Figure 10.4 provides a simple system for describing a behavior. If you were to collect this type of data for several instances of a behavior, you might see patterns that could be helpful in preventing it.

If there is a pattern in answers to any one of the questions above, you are one step closer to understanding the disruptive behavior's underlying cause and considering ways to prevent it. Sometimes simply acknowledging the cause to the student can go a long way:

- "I know that writing is a big challenge. Today I want you to see if you can write two words. Then you can work on your illustration."
- "Yesterday small-group time was hard. Today, if you feel frustrated, you can move to the take-a-break area and come back when you are ready."
- "In a few minutes we are going to end our centers time. I just want you to know that so you can get ready to stop, even though you are not finished. Tomorrow you can go back and work again."

Remember to rely on other members of your team to help you think through potential strategies to help an individual child learn to regulate his or her behavior or emotions. Just as you would seek help if you struggled to teach a decoding skill, a problem behavior is a teaching and learning opportunity. Your grade-level peers may have experience-tested routines to share, or you can seek the advice of special educators and school psychologists who can help you to implement evidence-based behavioral interventions. Also remember that families are your partners in the social and emotional development of their children (Epstein et al., 2008).

Summary

A well-managed classroom has a number of routines that are carefully selected and purposefully taught. That instruction typically includes a combination of physical modeling and practice and direct explanation, and only the modeling and practice fade over time. Continued explanation of procedures provides a safety net for students, especially those for whom self-regulation is challenging. It lets them know that you have set up a system for the next task, that they know what it is, and that it is time to implement it. Routines are worth the time they take to establish; they can be evaluated by simple data collection and personal introspection, and they can be modified if they are not working.

Child:	Date:

Describe the behavior for someone who did not witness it.

In what instructional or transitional contexts had the child been successful that day?

What was the instructional or transitional context of the behavior?

Would you judge that task in which you were engaging the student as simple or difficult for him or her?

What happened just before the student exhibited the behavior?

With what other students was the student interacting?

What actions did you take that did not work?

What actions did you take that worked?

Why do you think the student stopped the behavior?

FIGURE 10.4. Reflective log for understanding the context of disruptive behavior. From *Organizing the Early Literacy Classroom: How to Plan for Success and Reach Your Goals* by Sharon Walpole and Michael C. McKenna. Copyright © 2016 The Guilford Press. Permission to photocopy this figure is granted to purchasers of this book for personal use or use with individual students (see copyright page for details). Purchasers can download enlarged versions of this figure (see the box at the end of the table of contents).

CHAPTER 11

. . . .

Planning Communications with Families

GUIDING QUESTIONS

- Why is it important to involve families in the work of the school?
- In what ways can you encourage families to become involved?
- Why are some families reluctant or fearful of involvement?
- How can you be sure that you are communicating clearly with families?
- What are some effective opportunities for communicating?
- How can you contend with parents who are unresponsive or resistant?

We chose to title this chapter "planning communications" rather than "family involvement." Planning communications is something that every teacher can control. Family involvement, on the other hand, will be influenced by a variety of factors. One of them, though, is high-quality, inviting communications. We will see that "children benefit when meaningful connections are made between significant adults in their environment" (Semke & Sheridan, 2012, p. 23).

Understanding Why Family Involvement Is Vital

Despite rumors to the contrary, family involvement in children's K–12 education is actually increasing over time. It is particularly high in the early primary grades, and it includes two very different types of involvement—school-based involvement (e.g., meetings, events, and conferences) and home-based involvement (e.g., support for completing homework, regular bedtimes) (Choi, Chang, Kim, & Reio, 2015). It may be helpful to know that parents tend to think of family involvement as comprising what they do at home to ensure that children are ready for school in the morning while teachers may define involvement as parents' presence in school. It is important to consider and nurture both types of involvement (Smith, Wohlstetter, Kuzin, & De Pedro, 2011). You also may be disproportionately influenced to believe that parents are less involved overall because you know a particular family whose apparent lack of involvement seems to be affecting a child; it is helpful to understand how and why involvement is important, what barriers to involvement affect some families, and how to reach out through positive communications.

It would be unwise to ignore demographics in a discussion of family involvement. Affluent white families are typically more involved in school-based ways. They may have fewer barriers to overcome. Work schedules and transportation may not be challenges; language may not be a limitation; their own memories of school may be more positive. Poor and/or minority parents may face all of these barriers. Immigrant families may bring both assets and challenges: In spite of language challenges, they are more likely to be two-parent families, with strong and positive feelings about school and about their children's potential to succeed in life if they succeed in school (Sibley & Dearing, 2014).

To broaden our definition of family involvement, Epstein (2015) defines six types of involvement, described in Figure 11.1. You will see that they are actually a graduated set of partnerships among families, schools, and communities. Partnerships with families involve families as decision makers in schools.

Parent involvement in the first years of school has been studied for its immediate effects and its effects over time. Figure 11.2 provides an illustration. School efforts to reach out to parents increase their involvement in school. Both home environments and school experiences contribute to early literacy and math achievement. That early achievement influences children's attitudes about learning and

---

1. Families provide children a healthy and safe home environment.

2. Schools reach out to families with a variety of communications.

3. Family members come to school to attend meetings or provide help and support.

4. Family members help children with homework.

5. Family members serve on committees or boards to help make decisions for schools.

6. Family members, school representatives, and health and social service agencies share information and responsibility for services.

FIGURE 11.1. Epstein's (2011) types of collaborations.

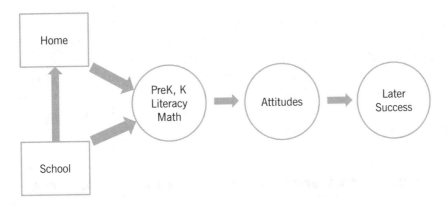

FIGURE 11.2. The relationship between family involvement and student achievement.

school. Their attitudes are related to their success as they get older. Researchers recommend that schools extend invitations and provide regular communication to families as part of their overall plan to support early academic achievement (Galindo & Sheldon, 2012).

The efforts to increase family involvement, particularly during the preschool years, can have effects on important early school outcomes. It's not enough to send books home. Measurable effects have been documented by the combination of high-quality instruction in school, access to print at home, and evening trainings during which parents are taught simple procedures for using books at home. These book reading trainings are realistic for most schools to host. They are large-group and led by teachers. Best yet, they seem to help close the achievement gap in important preschool skills (print concepts and language development) (Anthony, Williams, Zhang, Landry, & Dunkelberger, 2014).

One of the lessons that we have learned both from the professional literature and from practice is that effective teachers reach out to parents in ways that respect parent participation rather than demand it. In a seminal study of teachers and schools, family involvement was a characteristic of the most effective schools, but the take-home message is in the way it was measured. High levels of family involvement were credited to schools who *reached out more often and in more ways* rather than schools whose parents were more involved. Remember this: it is the number of invitations you send rather than the affirmative RSVPs you receive that truly counts. In the early primary years, three practices seem vital: sending books home for parents to share with children (including books in parents' home languages); sending brief, simply worded weekly newsletters from classrooms to help parents celebrate the week's accomplishments; and calls home to catch children being good (Taylor, Pearson, Clark, & Walpole, 2000).

Given the evidence that reaching out and communicating is important, why does it actually vary across classrooms? One reason is that many teachers face language barriers and don't have good strategies for connecting with immigrant families. Another is that teachers may simply feel that this is not their job, neglecting to consider that strong relationships with families may increase their effectiveness with improving academic and social outcomes. Communication is an important way to pay it forward with families; although it won't work every time, it will often create a shared commitment to a child that is more effective than when family and school function alone.

Keeping Literacy Talk Clear and Jargon Free

The tone of your communications with parents is important. Jargon that is only useful for teachers (e.g., phonemic segmentation) can easily be replaced by common language (e.g., learning to break words apart and spell them). Otherwise we risk alienating parents and communicating tacitly that they can no longer understand or contribute to their children's growth. Figure 11.3 provides a list of academic goals with some possible jargon-free language.

Curricular Goal	Jargon-Free Description
Oral Language	"We are working on listening and speaking skills this week. Ask your child about listening ears and looking eyes. Ask your child about taking turns when people talk. You can ask in English or in any language."
Storybook Reading	"We are learning that pictures in books have a lot of information. Ask your child to tell you about pictures in books or other places."
Alphabet Knowledge	"We are learning the letters and sounds. We talk about them every day. The children are getting confident and quick."
Phonemic Awareness	"We are learning that we can take words that we hear, break them apart, and write the sounds. Don't worry if your child's writing has mistakes. That's part of how we are learning together."
Assessments	"I will give some tests this week that will help me teach your child better. I will start small groups soon and that will help me teach your child more quickly. The tests help me understand just what to do."
Fluency	"We got a lot of reading and writing done this week! I am trying to make sure that all children get a lot of practice time every day. At home, if your child wants to read the same book over and over, that is perfectly fine. That's the kind of practice we do in school."
Content	"We have been learning about gardens this week. The children tell me that many families have flowers and plants and vegetables growing at home. See if your child can tell you anything new about the plants in your neighborhood."

FIGURE 11.3. Jargon-free descriptions of important curriculum goals.

Communicating in Multiple Ways

Think about the multiple ways communications affect you. If you had a text message from a supervisor to pop by the office, it would not evoke the same reaction as a formal letter with the same request. We must be careful to avoid situations where the only communications we have with families are formal summaries of test results or report cards. Relationships nurtured in advance of such formal communications make them less intimidating.

Home Visits

Many schools employ home visits as a welcoming strategy, especially for preschool or kindergarten children. Their power cannot be underestimated. But teachers or families may feel uncomfortable without some preparation. There are some common-sense ways to reduce anxiety. First, schedule the visits in advance at a time that is convenient for families. Allow them to change the venue to a public location, like a library, if they are reluctant to open their home. Second, bring a translator if one will be needed, or at least another colleague so that you are not entering a new place alone. And third, don't use the visit to fill out forms or explain complex school policies and procedures. Use it to build relationships.

We have worked with a preschool center initiating home visits to welcome Hispanic families. The school made a short video for all of the teachers to watch that clarified that the role of the home visit was to begin the relationship building that would continue throughout the year. The visits were centered on a very short discussion protocol, designed to provide and elicit information. A bilingual teacher or paraprofessional came to every visit. The teacher first told about his or her family, looking at the family rather than the translator, and the translator restated. The teacher then asked the family to tell about themselves. The teacher showed pictures of the school, including the bus for students with disabilities, the parent information room, and several typical daily events. The teacher left an inexpensive pad of paper and crayons and a book that the family could read together. The visit ended with sharing of contact information, including a card that could be hung on the refrigerator with the school phone number, the teacher's name, and a calendar.

Calls and Notes

We first learned about the power of positive phone calls while collecting data for a study of effective schools. We worked with two different principals whose main strategy for connecting with parents—especially the parents of the youngest students—involved picking up the phone. They began with a list of all students, seeking out two each day to actually observe in regular activities (lunch, recess, hallway). They collected a positive anecdote and called parents to tell it, either connecting by phone or leaving a message. The power of a 30-second message was palpable, they said. They left messages like this:

- "I saw your son on the playground today. He was king of the jungle gym. I know you would have been proud of him."
- "Your child shared her lunch with a child who was having a bad day. It really helped."

These positive calls set up relationships with families on which administrators and teachers could continue to build. This type of proactive calling is very different from the calls that most teachers tend to use to report academic or behavioral issues. This same approach could be extended to texting, provided you know a cell phone number and the parent's account enables them to receive texts.

Making calls home to all students, both to welcome them to your classroom and to check in periodically, is an essential strategy for all teachers who want to communicate with parents and invite them to be involved. Calls are more difficult when families are not fluent speakers of English, but are relying on a neighbor or an older sibling to take the call and then translate; this is a fine strategy as long as the communication is not about student achievement. Even better, using an Internet translating system, such as Google Translate or Bing Translator, to take a simple message, translate it into a family's home language, and then struggle through delivering it sends a very powerful message. "I respect your family's language and I know that it's hard to talk in a new language, but I'll try if you will!" (Chen, Kyle, & McIntyre, 2008).

Parent Conferences

Although parent conferences might appear to be the "traditional" route for family involvement, they can be intimidating for many families. We applaud the many schools that make the timing of conferences more flexible for working families. Early morning (before work) or evening (after work) slots for meetings respect the very real challenges families face when they have jobs with little or no flex time. We also think that for families dealing with challenging home lives, phone conferences must sometimes serve as a substitute for the traditional face-to-face conferences.

When parents are able to come to school, teachers can make parent conferences much more productive by defining them as opportunities for family members to understand their child's achievement relative to standards and to understand the teacher's efforts to provide individualized attention. Consider conferences as a chance to share what a child is doing and what you are doing to support his or her growth instead of an opportunity to direct home-based family involvement. You may find that families who understand what *you* are doing to help are more willing to ask you if there is anything that *they* can do to help.

Remember that children provide varying descriptions of school, often without any real information about day-to-day activities. Artifacts really help. A look at the classroom schedule, the child's desk and cubby, the morning procedures, and the child's journal provide a concrete picture for family members who send their children to school every day. Standards, too, can become more concrete if you can illustrate them with concrete examples. Think about gathering some samples of student writing (with names removed) from the beginning, middle, and end of the year to help parents know what sort of growth will be required. If you teach in first grade or second, gather texts to illustrate text difficulty in the same way.

Newsletters and Websites

If formal newsletters and websites are to be effective means of communication, they have to be accessible. The key is language and opportunity. Newsletters, if kept simple, actually can be translated. In fact, an urban charter school concerned with family involvement has its newsletter routinely translated into six languages (Smith et al., 2011).

Special Events

We may think of back-to-school nights or formal evening programming as the only way to bring parents into school, but that is simply not true. One easy way that schools can reach out to families is for school leaders to ride the school bus in the first week of school, bringing fruit or juice to the family members who wait with their children. This provides a welcoming presence on the bus, reducing anxiety for parents, and makes school personnel a regular part of the neighborhood where families live.

When families are invited to school, we must be ready to welcome them. Families may face barriers to attendance that can be removed. The best programs include transportation (employing the school bus) and child care for siblings. They provide food for families, extending the welcome. We know schools where parent pasta nights started small but quickly became full community events. We also have seen schools provide live translations via headsets so that families can listen in their home languages.

Researchers have been leveraging the power of families to design interventions for specific students that include home and school components. For example, young children with hyperactivity disorders can be more successful if programs include such collaborations, with parent trainings, home visits, and structured communications between home and school. Such work enhances both parenting skills and student success at school (Mautone et al., 2012).

Help with homework can be more complex than we anticipate for parents. We found it very interesting that a study of urban charter schools found that visits to school were encouraged and incentivized, but help with homework was actually an optional type of involvement. Schools provided parents evening trainings on how to help with homework if they wished, loaned families books and materials, and actively encouraged reading aloud, especially in the families' home languages (Smith et al., 2011). To us, such efforts seem both respectful of families and cultures and indicative of the mission of schooling.

Contending with Unresponsive and Resistant Parents

One of the hardest lessons that any teacher learns is not to judge families for their involvement. We urge you to consider walking a mile in a family member's shoes. Remember that family members were once students themselves, and their experience with schooling may have been negative. They may be struggling with finances and coping with daily responsibilities; they may have multiple children and adults in their care; they may not have access to cars or to public transportation. Parents in rural areas may be even less able to interact with teachers than their peers in urban or suburban areas (Semke & Sheridan, 2012).

For parents who are not willing or able to be involved in traditional ways, remember that you control the number and types of invitations that you provide. You cannot really know how those invitations are received. You should be most vigilant with families for whom involvement is most challenging.

Summary

Establishing lines of communication with the parents of your students is essential. This is sure to be a challenge with some families because of the various barriers they face. But it is a challenge worth pursuing. It is helpful to understand that involvement comes in a variety of forms and knowing what the options are can help you take a successful first step in reaching any family.

Regardless of the avenues you choose, a guiding principle at all times must be respect. Showing respect for a family's home language and cultural traditions is vitally important if you are to engage them as true partners in the education of their children. Respect also involves the language you use in communicating with parents. Avoiding technical jargon is especially important not only because it hampers getting your message across but because it may imply that parents are unable to understand the work of the school.

Finally, it is useful to keep in mind the variety of ways you can communicate with parents. You must think beyond the traditional view of the teacher–parent conference and consider other opportunities. These include home visits, phone calls, text messages, notes, newsletters, websites, and special events.

Despite all of these efforts, there are likely to be parents you simply cannot reach. Your responsibility only extends so far, but it must include continuing attempts to get through. Don't give up! Eventually, you may be rewarded for your efforts.

References

Anthony, J. J., Williams, J. M., Zhang, Z., Landry, S. H., & Dunkelberger, M. J. (2014). Experimental evaluation of the value added by Raising a Reader and supplemental parent training in shared reading. *Early Education and Development, 25*, 493–514.

Bear, D. R., Invernizzi, M., Templeton, S., & Johnson, F. (2015). *Words their way: Word study for phonics, vocabulary, and spelling instruction* (5th ed.). Upper Saddle River, NJ: Pearson/Prentice Hall.

Beck, I. L., McKeown, M. G., & Kucan, L. (2008). *Creating robust vocabulary: Frequently asked questions and extended examples.* New York: Guilford Press.

Black, P., & Wiliam, D. (1998). Assessment and classroom learning. *Assessment in Education: Principles, Policy, and Practice, 5*(1), 7–74.

Board of Directors, International Reading Association. (2000). *Teaching all children to read: The roles of the reading specialist (A position statement of the International Reading Association).* Newark, DE: International Reading Association.

Board of Directors, International Reading Association. (2004). *The role and qualifications of the reading coach in the United States: A position statement of the International Reading Association.* Newark, DE: International Reading Association.

Brophy, J. (1986). Principles for conducting first grade reading group instruction. In J. V. Hoffman (Ed.), *Effective teaching of reading: Research and practice* (pp. 53–84). Newark, DE: International Reading Association.

Brown, K. J. (1999). What kind of text—for whom and when?: Textual scaffolding for beginning readers. *The Reading Teacher, 53*, 292–307.

Chen, C., Kyle, D. W., & McIntyre, E. (2008). Helping teachers work effectively with English language learners and their families. *School Community Journal, 18*, 7–20.

Choi, N., Chang, M., Kim, S., & Reio, T. G. (2015). A structural model of parent involvement with demographic and academic variables. *Psychology in the Schools, 52*, 154–167.

Coker, D. L., & Ritchey, K. D. (2015). *Teaching beginning writers.* New York: Guilford Press.

Conley, M. W. (2005). *Connecting standards and assessment through literacy.* Boston: Pearson.

Cooper, O., & Bray, M. (2011). School library media specialist-teacher collaboration: Characteristics, challenges, opportunities. *Techtrends: Linking Research and Practice to Improve Learning, 55,* 48–55.

Council for Exceptional Children. (2013). The Council for Exceptional Children's Position on Special Education Teacher Evaluation. *Teaching Exceptional Children, 45*(3), 73–76.

Covey, S. (1989). *The seven habits of highly effective people.* New York: Simon and Schuster.

Duke, N. K. (2000). 3.6 minutes per day: The scarcity of informational texts in first grade. *Reading Research Quarterly, 35,* 202–224.

Duke, N. K. (2003). *Reading and writing informational text in the primary grades: Research-based practices.* New York: Scholastic.

Epstein, J. L. (2015). *School, family, and community partnerships: Preparing educators and improving schools* (2nd ed.). Philadelphia: Westview Press.

Epstein, M., Atkins, M., Cullinan, D., Kutash, K., & Weaver, R. (2008). *Reducing behavior problems in the elementary school classroom: A practice guide* (NCEE No. 2008-012). Washington, DC: National Center for Education Evaluation and Regional Assistance, Institute of Education Sciences, U.S. Department of Education. Retrieved from *http:// ies.ed.gov/ncee/wwc/publications/practiceguides.*

Ezell, H. K., & Justice, L. M. (2005). *Shared storybook reading: Building young children's language and emergent literacy skills.* Baltimore: Brookes.

Fitzgerald, J., Elmore, J., Koons, H., Hiebert, E. H., Bowen, K., Sanford-Moore, E. E., et al. (2015). Important text characteristics for early-grades text complexity. *Journal of Educational Psychology, 107,* 4–29.

Fountas, I. C., & Pinnell, G. S. (1996). *Guided reading: Good first teaching for all children.* Portsmouth, NH: Heinemann.

Friend, M., Embury, D. C., & Clarke, L. (2015). Co-teaching versus apprentice teaching: An analysis of similarities and differences. *Teacher Education and Special Education, 38,* 79–87.

Galindo, C., & Sheldon, S. B. (2012). School and home connections and children's kindergarten achievement gains: The mediating role of family involvement. *Early Childhood Research Quarterly, 27,* 90–103.

Goddard, R. D., Hoy, W. K., & Hoy, A. W. (2000). Collective teacher efficacy: Its meaning, measure, and impact on student achievement. *American Educational Research Journal, 37,* 479–507.

Graham, S., Bollinger, A., Booth Olson, C., D'Aoust, C., MacArthur, C., McCutchen, D., et al. (2012). *Teaching elementary school students to be effective writers: A practice guide* (NCEE No. 2012-4058). Washington, DC: National Center for Education Evaluation and Regional Assistance, Institute of Education Sciences, U.S. Department of Education. Retrieved from *http://ies.ed.gov/ncee/wwc/publications_reviews. aspx#pubsearch.*

Guskey, T. R., & Bailey, J. M. (2010). *Developing standards-based report cards.* Thousand Oaks, CA: Corwin.

Guskey, T. R., & Jung, L. A. (2013). *Answers to essential questions about standards, assessments, grading, and reporting.* Thousand Oaks, CA: Corwin Press.

Halladay, J. L., & Duke, N. K. (2013). Informational text and the Common Core State Standards. In S. B. Neuman & L. B. Gambrell (Eds.), *Quality reading instruction in the age of Common Core Standards* (pp. 44–58). Newark, DE: International Reading Association.

Harn, W. E., Bradshaw, M. L., & Ogletree, B. T. (1999). The speech–language pathologist in the schools: Changing roles. *Intervention in School and Clinic, 34,* 163–169.

Hayes, L., & Flanigan, K. (2014). *Developing word recognition.* New York: Guilford Press.

Hoffman, J. L., Paciga, K. A., & Teale, W. H. (2014). *Common Core State Standards and early childhood literacy instruction: Confusions and conclusions* (UIC Center for Literacy Research Paper). Chicago: University of Illinois at Chicago Center for Literacy.

Hoffman, J. V., Sailors, M., Duffy, G. R., & Beretvas, S. N. (2004). The effective elementary classroom literacy environment: Examining the validity of the TEX-IN3 observation system. *Journal of Literacy Research, 36,* 303–334.

Johnston, M. P. (2015). Blurred lines: The school librarian and the instructional technology specialist. *Techtrends: Linking Research and Practice to Improve Learning, 59,* 17–26.

Jones, S. M., Bailey, R., & Jacob, R. (2014). Social–emotional learning is essential to classroom management. *Phi Delta Kappan, 96,* 19–24.

Joyce, B., & Showers, B. (2002). *Student achievement through staff development* (3rd ed.). Alexandria, VA: ASCD.

Jung, L. A., & Guskey, T. R. (2012). *Grading exceptional and struggling learners.* Thousand Oaks, CA: Corwin Press.

Kuhn, M. R., & Levy, L. (2015). *Developing fluent readers: Teaching fluency as a foundational skill.* New York: Guilford Press.

Lane, H. B., Pullen, P. C., & Eisele, M. R. (2002). Preventing reading failure: Phonological awareness assessment and instruction. *Preventing School Failure, 46,* 101–110.

Lleras, C., & Rangel, C. (2009). Ability grouping practices in elementary school and African American/Hispanic achievement. *American Journal of Education, 115,* 279–304.

Lonigan, C. J., & Whitehurst, G. J. (1998). Relative efficacy of parent and teacher involvement in a shared-reading intervention for preschool children from low-income backgrounds. *Early Childhood Research Quarterly, 17,* 265–292.

MacKeracher, D. (2004). *Making sense of adult learning* (2nd ed.). Toronto: University of Toronto Press.

Mautone, J. A., Marshall, S. A., Sharman, J., Eiraldi, R. B., Jawad, A. F., & Power, T. J. (2012). Development of a family-school intervention for young children with attention deficit hyperactivity disorder. *School Psychology Review, 41,* 447–466.

McGee, L. M., & Richgels, D. J. (2014). *Designing early literacy programs: Differentiated instruction in preschool and kindergarten* (2nd ed.). New York: Guilford Press.

Mcintosh, C. E., Thomas, C. M., & Maughan, E. (2015). Introduction to the special issue: Increasing the collaboration between school nurses and school personnel. *Psychology in the Schools, 52,* 631–634.

McKenna, M. C., Conradi, K., Young, C. A., & Jang, B. G. (2013). Technology and the

Common Core Standards. In L. M. Morrow, T. Shanahan, & K. K. Wixson (Eds.), *Teaching with the Common Core Standards for English language arts, PreK–2* (pp. 152–169). New York: Guilford Press.

McKenna, M. C., & Stahl, K. A. D. (2015). *Assessment for reading instruction* (3rd ed.). New York: Guilford Press.

McKenna, M. C., & Walpole, S. (2005). How well does assessment inform our reading instruction? *The Reading Teacher, 59,* 84–86.

McKenna, M. C., & Walpole, S. (2008). *The literacy coaching challenge: Models and methods for grades K–8.* New York: Guilford Press.

McLaughlin, M., & Overturf, B. J. (2012). The Common Core: Insights into the K–5 standards. *The Reading Teacher, 66,* 153–164.

Mesmer, H. A. E., Mesmer, E., & Jones, J. (2014). *Reading intervention in the primary grades: A common-sense guide to RTI.* New York: Guilford Press.

Morrow, L. M. (1990). Preparing the classroom environment to promote literacy during play. *Early Childhood Research Quarterly, 5,* 537–554.

Morrow, L. M. (2002). *The literacy center: Contexts for reading and writing* (2nd ed.). Portland, ME: Stenhouse.

Morrow, L. M. (2014). *Literacy development in the early years: Helping children read and write* (8th ed.). Boston: Pearson Education.

Muñoz, M. A., & Guskey, T. R. (2015). Standards-based grading and reporting will improve education. *Phi Delta Kappan, 96*(7), 64–68.

National Center for Education Statistics. (2005). School and Staffing Survey. *https://nces.ed.gov/surveys/sass/tables/sass0708_035_s1s.asp.*

National Governors Association Center for Best Practices & Council of Chief State School Officers. (2010). *Common Core State Standards for English language arts and literacy in history/social studies, science, and technical subjects.* Washington, DC: Author. Available at *www.corestandards.org/ELA-Literacy.*

Neuman, S. B., & Gambrell, L. B. (2013). Challenges and opportunities in the implementation of Common Core State Standards. In S. B. Neuman & L. B. Gambrell (Eds.), *Quality reading instruction in the age of Common Core Standards* (pp. 1–12). Newark, DE: International Reading Association.

Neuman, S. B., & Roskos, K. (1992). Literacy objects as cultural tools: Effects on children's literacy behaviors in play. *Reading Research Quarterly, 27,* 202–225.

Oliver, R. M., Wehby, J. J., & Nelson, J. R. (2015). Helping teachers maintain classroom management practices using a self-monitoring checklist. *Teaching and Teacher Education, 51,* 113–120.

Paris, S. G. (2005). Reinterpreting the development of reading skills. *Reading Research Quarterly, 40,* 184–202.

Pas, E. T., Bradshaw, C. P., & Hershfeldt, P. A. (2012). Teacher- and school-level predictors of teacher efficacy and burnout: Identifying potential areas for support. *Journal of School Psychology, 50,* 129–145.

Pawan, F., & Ortloff, J. H. (2011). Sustaining collaboration: English-as-a-second-language, and content-area teachers. *Teaching and Teacher Education, 27,* 463–471.

Reutzel, D. R., & Wolfersberger, M. E. (1996). An environmental impact statement:

Designing supportive literacy classrooms for young children. *Reading Horizons, 36,* 266–282.

Rivkin, S. G., Hanushek, E. A., & Kain, A. F. (2005). Teachers, schools, and academic achievement. *Econometrica, 73,* 417–458.

Robertson-Craft, C., & Duckworth, A. L. (2014). True grit: Trait-level perseverance and passion for long-term goals predicts effectiveness and retention among novice teachers. *Teachers College Record, 116,* 1–27.

Samuels, S. J. (1979). The method of repeated readings. *The Reading Teacher, 32,* 403–408.

Semke, C. A., & Sheridan, S. M. (2012). Family-school connections in rural educational settings: A systematic review of the empirical literature. *School Community Journal, 22,* 21–47.

Shanahan, T. (2015, July 28). Report cards and standards (Blog post). Shanahanonliteracy. Available at *www.shanahanonliteracy.com/2015/07/report-cards-and-standards. html.*

Showers, B., & Joyce, B. (1996). The evolution of peer coaching. *Educational Leadership, 53*(6), 12–16.

Sibley, E., & Dearing, E. (2014). Family educational involvement and child achievement in early elementary school for American-born and immigrant families. *Psychology in the Schools, 51,* 814–831.

Silverman, R., & Hartranft, A. M. (2015). *Developing vocabulary and oral language in young children.* New York: Guilford Press.

Smith, J., Wohlstetter, P., Kuzin, C. A., & De Pedro, K. (2011). Parent involvement in urban charter schools: New strategies for increasing participation. *School Community Journal, 21,* 71–94.

Smith, M. W., Dickinson, D. K., Sangeorge, A., & Anastasopoulos, L. (2002). *Early Language and Literacy Classroom Observation (ELLCO) toolkit.* Baltimore: Brookes.

Stahl, K. A. D., & García, G. E. (2015). *Developing reading comprehension: Effective instruction for all students in PreK–2.* New York: Guilford Press.

Stahl, K. A. D., & McKenna, M. C. (2013). *Reading assessment in an RTI framework.* New York: Guilford Press.

Stahl, S. A., Kuhn, M. R., & Pickle, J. M. (1999). An educational model of assessment and targeted instruction for children with reading problems. In D. H. Evensen & P. Mosenthal (Eds.), *Reconsidering the role of the reading clinic in a new age of literacy* (pp. 249–272). Stamford, CT: JAI Press.

Strickland, D. (2013). Linking early literacy research and the Common Core State Standards. In S. B. Neuman & L. B. Gambrell (Eds.), *Quality reading instruction in the age of Common Core Standards* (pp. 13–25). Newark, DE: International Reading Association.

Swan, G. M., Guskey, T. R., & Jung, L. A. (2014). Parents' and teachers' perceptions of standards-based and traditional report cards. *Educational Assessment, Evaluation and Accountability, 26,* 289–299.

Swanson, E., Vaughn, S., Wanzek, J., Petscher, Y., Heckert, J., Cavanaugh, C., et al. (2011). A synthesis of read-aloud interventions on early reading outcomes among preschool through third graders at risk for reading difficulties. *Journal of Learning Disabilities,* *44,* 258–275.

Taylor, B. M., Pearson, P. D., Clark, K. F., & Walpole, S. (2000). Effective schools and accomplished teachers: Lessons about primary-grade reading instruction in low-income schools. *Elementary School Journal, 101,* 121–165.

Tomlinson, C. A., & Moon, T. R. (2013). *Assessment and student success in a differentiated classroom.* Alexandria, VA: ASCD.

Turbill, J., & Murray, J. (2006). Early literacy and new technologies in Australian schools: Policy, research, and practice. In M. C. McKenna, L. D. Labbo, R. Kieffer, & D. Reinking (Eds.), *International handbook of literacy and technology* (Vol. 2, pp. 93–108). Mahwah, NJ: Erlbaum.

Walpole, S., & McKenna, M. C. (2009). *How to plan differentiated reading instruction: Resources for grades K–3.* New York: Guilford Press.

Walpole, S., & McKenna, M. C. (2013). *The literacy coach's handbook* (2nd ed.): *A guide to research-based practice.* New York: Guilford Press.

Walpole, S., McKenna, M. C., & Philippakos, Z. (2011). *Differentiated reading instruction in grades 4 and 5: Strategies and resources.* New York: Guilford Press.

Wiggins, G. (1994). Toward better report cards. *Educational Leadership, 52*(2), 28–37.

Willingham, D. T., & Lovette, G. E. (2014, September 26). Can reading comprehension be taught? *Teachers College Record.* Retrieved from *http://tcrecord.org/Content. asp?ContentID=17701.*

Wohlwend, K. E. (2010). A is for avatar: Young children in literacy 2.0 worlds and literacy 1.0 schools. *Language Arts, 88,* 144–152.

Wolfersberger, M. E., Reutzel, D. R., Sudweeks, R., & Fawson, P. C. (2004). Developing and validating the Classroom Literacy Environmental Profile (CLEP): A tool for examining the "print richness" of early childhood and elementary classrooms. *Journal of Literacy Research, 36,* 211–272.

Young, M. H., & Balli, S. J. (2014). Gifted and talented education (GATE). *Gifted Child Today, 37,* 236–246.

Index

Note: *f* or *t* following a page number indicates a figure or a table.

129